"...the book is an excellent presentation of a historical district. Most of the photographs were supplied by long-time residents of the area. The text is the result of Wilson's thorough research of a vast collection of contemporary newspapers and interviews. This use of written and oral history has enabled Wilson to put together a very readable, comprehensive history of the area.

"Without trying to portray a "Wild West" image, Wilson has produced a realistic picture of the West."

John Norwood in *True West*

"It is one of the more useful of several locally published books that have accumulated on my desk."

James E. Cook, *The Arizona Republic*

"...Wilson's account of the exploration and mining of the southern part of Arizona's Bradshaw Mountains is thorough. Well-done local history...."

W. David Laird in *Books of the Southwest*

"...golden nuggets of history so tantalizing you can hardly put down the paper they're written on.

"Apache ambushes, gold rushes, miners' feuds and scores of other tales compose the portrait of the Brashaw Mountains in Bruce M. Wilson's newly published book, *Crown King and the Southern Bradshaws: A Complete History.*"

Groom Creek Chronicle

Crown King and the Southern Bradshaws: A Complete History

by
Bruce M. Wilson

Crown King Press

Mesa, Arizona

Copyright 1990 by Bruce M. Wilson

Publisher's Cataloging in Publication Data

Wilson, Bruce M.
   Crown King and the southern Bradshaws: a complete history

   Bibliography: p.
   Includes index
     1. Bradshaw Mountains Region (Ariz.) x History.
     2. Yavapai County (Ariz.) x History, Local.
     3. Cities and towns, Ruined, extinct, etc. z Arizona z Yavapai
     4. Crown King (Ariz.) x History.

Library of Congress Card Number: 90-83323

ISBN: 0-9627573-0-6

Second Printing - 1991

Printed in the United States of America

Front cover photo: *Crown King sometime between 1916 & 1927.* Courtesy Crown King Saloon
Back cover photo by Jan Wilson

Dedicated to my wife, Jan, with whom I shared many
wonderful years in Crown King

Table of Contents

Acknowledgements

I particularly want to thank the many Bradshaw old-timers who provided me with the information, stories, and photographs that give flesh to any history. They include: Tony and Abbie Nelson, Don Van Tilborg, Grant "Butch" Van Tilborg, Elsie Van Tilborg, Frances Nelson Pickett, Vernon Martin, Morse Whitley, Paul Turley and Lynn Clifford, Ray Singer, Bob and Pat Schmidt, Charles "Camp" and Lynn Armer, and Scott Burgess. Thanks to Sue Hite, at the Crown King Public Library, for her help. I also want to thank Mary Ann Sokol for her valuable help in proofreading the final draft.

I owe a great deal to Susie Sato and the staff at the Arizona Historical Foundation at ASU for their kind and patient help. Besides the individuals mentioned above, I also received photographs from the Sharlot Hall Museum in Prescott, the Crown King Saloon, the Arizona Historical Foundation, and the Prescott National Forest. Finally, I highly recommend the book, *Ghost Railroads of Central Arizona* by John Sayre, which contains a lot of information about the Bradshaws, and which I used as my main source for the chapters on Cleator and Middelton.

Finally, thanks to my wife Jan for her understanding and help through the many years that I have been researching and writing this history.

Preface

Ever since I first visited the Crown King area about twenty-five years ago I have had a fascination with and love for this out-of-the way corner of Arizona. I was amazed at how remote the Bradshaw Mountains seemed, even though they are within one hundred miles of Phoenix. This is mainly due to thirty miles of often-rough dirt road between Crown King and the nearest paved road.

After I was discharged from the Army and was married, my wife, Jan, and I both realized that we were not ready to settle into city life and we applied to the U.S. Forest Service as lookouts. To my delight, we were hired by the Prescott National Forest to man Horsethief Lookout on the Crown King Ranger District. For the next eight years, 1972 through 1979, Crown King was our home base, and we eventually bought a home there. My interest in the history of the area was heightened by the fact that our house had been built as a bunkhouse for railroad workers in 1904. While working as foreman of the recreation crew on the District, I volunteered to research and create a slide show on the history of the Crown King area. Doing research for the slide show was fascinating, and I was surprised at how little in-depth work had been done on an area that had such a great impact on the history of early Arizona. I left the Forest Service when the Crown King Ranger District was disbanded in 1979, and a couple of years later I decided to expand the text of my slide show into a complete history. I have been reading old newspapers, taking pictures, and talking to Bradshaw old-timers for the last seven years. I found that my familiarity with the area (there are few parts of the Bradshaws that I have not been to) and my friendship with most Bradshaw residents made it much easier for me to write this book than it would have been for an outsider to do so.

My wife and I now live in Mesa, but we still have our house in Crown King, which we visit frequently, as well as many friends there, both old and new. I hope that this book succeeds in giving Crown King a well-deserved place among the more important social and economic centers of early Arizona. I also hope that it will arouse an affection and respect for this beautiful and unique part of Arizona, which probably has more authentic old-west flavor than any other area in the state.

The Southern Bradshaws 1865 - 1900

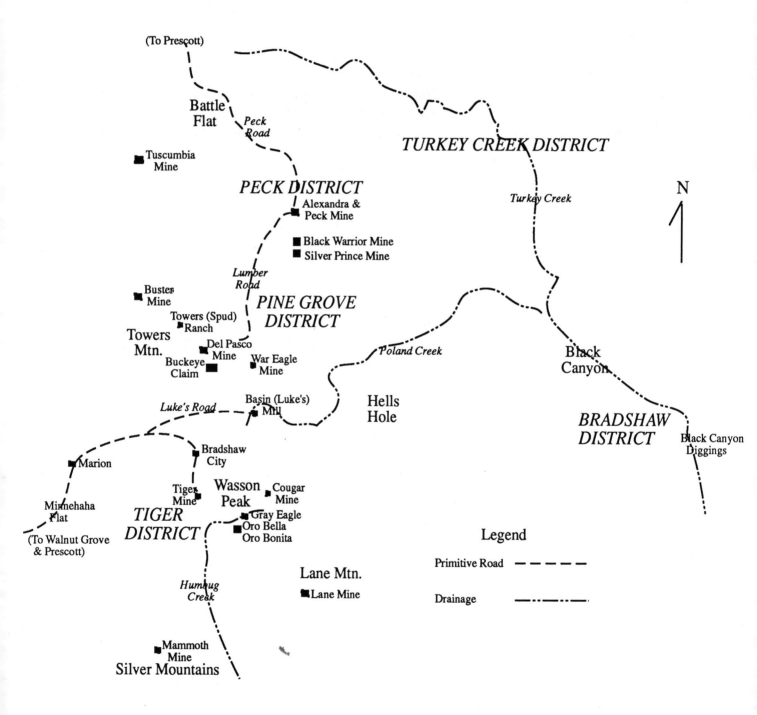

(To Prescott)

Battle Flat

Peck Road

TURKEY CREEK DISTRICT

Tuscumbia Mine

PECK DISTRICT

Turkey Creek

Alexandra & Peck Mine

■ Black Warrior Mine
■ Silver Prince Mine

Lumber Road

PINE GROVE DISTRICT

Buster Mine

Towers (Spud) Ranch

Towers Mtn.

Del Pasco Mine

Buckeye Claim

War Eagle Mine

Poland Creek

Black Canyon

Hells Hole

Luke's Road

Basin (Luke's) Mill

BRADSHAW DISTRICT

Black Canyon Diggings

Marion

Bradshaw City

Minnehaha Flat

Tiger Mine

Wasson Peak

Cougar Mine

TIGER DISTRICT

Gray Eagle
Oro Bella
Oro Bonita

(To Walnut Grove & Prescott)

Humbug Creek

Lane Mtn.

■ Lane Mine

Legend

Primitive Road   – – – – –

Drainage   —··—··—

Mammoth Mine

Silver Mountains

N

The Crown King Area
in the Twentieth Century

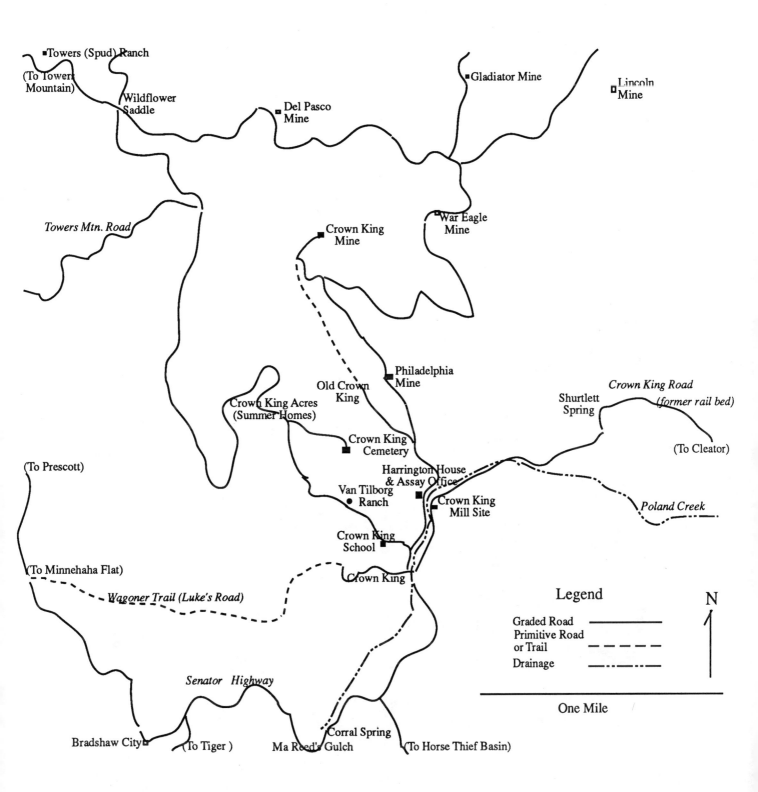

Towers (Spud) Ranch

(To Towers Mountain)

Wildflower Saddle

Del Pasco Mine

Gladiator Mine

Lincoln Mine

Towers Mtn. Road

War Eagle Mine

Crown King Mine

Philadelphia Mine

Old Crown King

Crown King Road
(former rail bed)

Shurtlett Spring

Crown King Acres
(Summer Homes)

(To Cleator)

(To Prescott)

Crown King Cemetery

Harrington House
& Assay Office

Van Tilborg Ranch

Crown King Mill Site

Poland Creek

Crown King School

(To Minnehaha Flat)

Crown King

Wagoner Trail (Luke's Road)

Legend

N

Graded Road

Primitive Road or Trail

Drainage

One Mile

Senator Highway

Bradshaw City

(To Tiger)

Ma Reed's Gulch

Corral Spring

(To Horse Thief Basin)

Chapter One:
The First Inhabitants

Archeologists identify the first inhabitants of the Bradshaw Mountains as relatives, or remnants, of the Hohokam Indians, who built canals and settlements in the Gila and Salt River Valleys. It is believed that Hohokams from the Agua Fria River area colonized the Bradshaws about 1100 A.D.

They used drainage bottoms and floodplains for growing crops, and built simple dwellings on nearby higher ground. They constructed pithouses, hilltop pueblos, and small "forts" on peaks with wide views to provide warning of enemy intrusion. An easily accessible example of such a fort is East Fort, to the east of Horse Thief Basin overlooking Black Canyon.

Climatic changes were one probable cause for the original colonization of the Bradshaws by the Hohokam, and were also a probable cause for their abandonment about 1300 A.D. The mountains were left to the Yavapai Indians and, much later, to the wandering Apaches. It was the Bradshaws' reputation as a stronghold for hostile Indians that kept white men out of the area for years.

East Fort, a prehistoric native American lookout point, located on a high ridge east of Horse Thief Basin. It has a magnificent view of Black Canyon.
Courtesy Crown King Saloon

Chapter Two:
The First American Incursions

The Ehrenberg Ferry across the Colorado River, established by William Bradshaw
and William Werringer in 1862. Courtesy Arizona Historical Foundation

The first known party of Anglos to enter the area was a small group of miners led by William Bradshaw. They did not actually penetrate the mountain range, but confined themselves to placering on Black Canyon and Turkey Creeks on the east side of the range. According to an old topographic map, Black Canyon begins south of the point where Poland Creek flows into Turkey Creek. The area was first worked by Mexicans who built arrastras, which were circular grooves in the ground lined with flat stones. Raw ore was placed in the grooves and large stones were dragged around the circle, usually by animals such as horses or oxen, to break down the ore. In two years they extracted $35,000 in gold. The Mexicans were eventually forced out by the Apaches. The success of the Mexican miners attracted Bradshaw, who led about fifty men from the Weaver diggings to these new placering grounds in 1863.

William D. Bradshaw was born in North Carolina in 1826. His father, Christopher, had migrated from Wales, and had fought in the Revolutionary War. The family, which included five sons and seven daughters, moved to Missouri in 1845. Once there, William and three of his brothers continued west. William went to California where he served as a Lieutenant in Fremont's California Battalion and claimed to be one of the original "Bear Flaggers." In 1862 he established a ferry across the Colorado at Ehrenberg with William Werringer. He quit the ferry to follow Captain Walker to central Arizona. In a letter printed in the *San Francisco Bulletin*, Bradshaw wrote: "I started a few days after Capt. Walker and Weaver and overtook them two days south of William's Fork, nearly at the mines. The next day after our arrival, I went out across the country and discovered a gulch, eastward, out of which I obtained in four days labor, 28 ounces and $12. This gulch is called Indians Gulch. Nine persons took up the ground between Antelope and Indian Creek. They have taken out as high as five pounds per day to the hand. I obtained a claim just above them, from which I obtained two dollars to the pan. Our grub is getting scarce, so I left what provisions we had with my partner, and arrived here in four days and a half. I have been a miner in California for 14 years, and I believe that these diggings are as good, or better than any I have ever seen..."[1] It is not certain that this is an account of his expedition to Black Canyon, but it took place in the same time period and was in the same approximate vicinity. A biographer of Bradshaw's maintains that his party only reached the western side of the mountains that now bear his name, and that he never got as far as the rich Black Canyon placers. However, Daniel Conner, one of the members of the original Walker expedition, wrote that he followed Bradshaw to the Turkey Creek diggings and gave the following account: "A more disgusted set of men never before sent on a fool's errand. This was a new land and looked at (sic) though it had never contained any human souls...

"These hills and rocks echoes back that day the first horrible oaths expressed in the English language that ever graced this hitherto sterile and graceless quarter. This trip served only to name a mountain near Turkey Creek. Bradshaw Mountain retains its name. These disappointed men soon scattered away in squads and left the region as we found it..."2

Bradshaw ran for the First Territorial Legislature in 1864 and got the least number of votes of any candidate. He also ran as the Democratic candidate for territorial representative to Congress, but lost to C. D. Poston, known as the "father of Arizona." He returned to La Paz where he committed suicide in December, 1864, while drunk, by nearly severing his head with a carpenter's draw knife. Bradshaw's brother, Isaac, was an active miner in the area for many years, but was not mentioned as one of the original Bradshaw party. He was said to have run the Colorado ferry while his brother prospected.

Interest in the area continued, however, and the establishment of the Bradshaw Mining District was announced in the Prescott *Miner* of September 21, 1864. The meeting that established the district was held on September 14, and was presided over by a Mr. Moore, with G. M. Whiting acting as Secretary. The district was to be ten miles square and named "in honor of the Bradshaw brothers, who brought the region to notice last autumn."3

Max Solomon was named president of the District and a town site was selected and named Montezuma. There was reported to be sixty Mexicans and twenty-five Americans working the placer claims with rockers. The gold was said to be of superior quality with large nuggets worth fifteen dollars. Shafts were up to eighteen feet deep.

Eventually the claims were abandoned because of Indian interference, as well as the difficulty of getting supplies to this isolated area. The only wood available for the construction of sluices lay high on the slopes of the Bradshaws.

In August, 1868, another party was raised to reopen the "Bradshaw Diggings," this time led by William Bradshaw's brother Ike (Isaac) and a Judge Flowers. Bradshaw and Flowers returned from Black Canyon, having left ten or eleven miners working the creek. Excitement was high about the area again and the *Weekly Arizona Miner* reported that: "...about thirty single men, and one family have arrived from the East and most of the men are preparing to go to the Black Canyon Diggings, Bradshaw District where, in less that two months, there will be a hundred miners."4 "Two or three men were in town endeavoring to raise a party to go to the south side of the Bradshaw Mountains, but find it an up-hill business, as almost all the miners hereabouts are stack after Black Canyon."5 By the middle of January, 1869, the rush to Black Canyon was continuing with over a hundred men already there. Wormser & Co., a Prescott merchant, considered opening a branch there. Lumber was hauled from Prescott rather than gathered from the pine forests six miles away. The weather was reported to be good all year. By late January, there were six companies of miners at Black Canyon. No one was expected to get rich, but miners could make four to ten dollars a day. The Poland party expected to make twenty dollars a day as soon as their ditch was completed. However, by April, most of the miners had left the district because of the high cost of transporting provisions to the diggings. Many were anxious to return, but the Prescott *Miner* suggested that, in spite of the richness of the placers, it would be sometime before they could be worked successfully. "Large parties cannot agree among themselves, and small parties dare not stop long in one place and work on account of the Indians."6 In early 1870, the paper reported that "...a party of prospectors from Walnut Grove took a trip around Bradshaw Mountains and found both gold and Indians. The Indians showed themselves on the top of the peaks sung out (sic) that they were 'Apache Mohaves, and good'. If devils are good, so are the villainous Indians why (sic) style themselves Apache Mohaves."7 By March, 1870, there were fifteen to twenty miners placering in the Black Canyon area. There was also mention of about twenty miners building arrastras to work quartz lodes higher up Black Canyon in the Pine Grove District. This is one of the first reports of white men in the Bradshaw Mountains themselves. The Pine Grove District includes Bradshaw Basin, the area in which Crown King is now located.

The Turkey Creek Mining District was also established at this time, just to the north of the original Bradshaw District. A meeting was held on August 10, 1864, with Charles Taylor as president. Taylor was a member of the original Walker expedition who later settled in Minnehaha Flat on the west side of the Bradshaws. The Turkey Creek District boundaries extended from the head of Lynx and Turkey Creeks down the Agua Fria, over to Pine Mountain, and across to the Hassayampa River.

In 1867, several groups of miners prospected in the Silver Mountain, Humbug and Oak Creek areas to the south and west of the Bradshaw range. Hinton, in his *Handbook to Arizona*, says that Mexicans had placered in this area for several seasons prior to 1864. The Prescott *Miner* reported a stampede of miners headed for Silver Mountain on Oak Creek. Horses, flour, bacon and sugar were in great demand in Prescott as miners headed for the new strike. Floats were rumored to go as high as $1,700 per ton. By May, 1868, most of the prospectors had returned, having found ore, but not ore as rich as they had hoped. A Mr. Cole was placering at the head of Humbug Creek, the future site of the Oro Bella mine, and getting ore at fifteen cents to the pan. Another expedition was planned. In early 1870, a prospector reported finding good placer locations in the creeks and ravines on the west side of the Bradshaws in the Oak and Humbug Creek areas. "It is a brushy country and contains plenty of game, --such as bear, deer, and Indians."8

One of the most exciting events in the history of the Bradshaws took place in 1864 when five prospectors camped in a place that was to be named Battle Flat as a result of their desperate fight with a large band of Indians. Fred Henry, Stuart N. Wall, DeMarion Scott, Samuel Herron, and Frank Binkley camped for the night on a flat between the north and south branches of the Bradshaw mountains. They spread their blankets near the trail and went to sleep, neglecting to post a guard. During the night, a band of fifty or more Apaches discovered them and stole their horses. The Indians then surrounded the men and quietly threw up rock fortifications from behind which to attack the men at dawn. They were within twenty feet of the sleeping prospectors when one of them woke up and, suspecting that something was wrong, drew his weapon and began to fire. The Indians fired back, wounding all five men before retreating to their barricades. The five surrounded themselves with their packs and saddles, and beat back attack after attack. The men were all wounded severely. Binkley had lost an eye and another had a broken leg. They managed to work themselves up onto a small nearby ridge but were too weak to go any farther. Gradually the Indians began to lose interest after many of their own were killed or wounded. By two o'clock in the afternoon all the Indians except one had left to eat horseflesh or tend the wounded. The final Indian was killed as he tried to hit one of the party over the head with a rock. Luckily, one of the other five was alert enough to spot the Indian and finish him off with a shotgun. That was the last shot of the battle. After nightfall, Henry and Binkley, the strongest of the group, worked their way out of the flat and managed to get to Walnut Grove by noon of the following day. A rescue party of fifteen men returned to the site of the battle and found the blood-stained ground and fourteen dead Indians piled in preparation for cremation. They found the remaining three men, two of whom were unconscious, and brought them back to Walnut Grove, where one of them died. It was a desperate battle and a miraculous escape.

Chapter Three:
The Del Pasco Mine

The first big strike that really stirred excitement about the Bradshaws was the discovery of the Del Pasco mine on July 4, 1870. The Del Pasco is located on the ridge to the northeast of Crown King, between the town's present location and Towers Mountain. The discoverers of the Del Pasco were Jackson McCracken, James Fine, Charley Taylor and T.G. Hogle. They arrived in Prescott a few days after their discovery with samples of ore that prompted the *Miner* to proclaim the Bradshaws as one of the richest districts on the coast. The group stocked up with tools and provisions and headed back to their bonanza, followed by other prospectors who wanted to get in on the action. Charley Taylor was mentioned in Chapter Two regarding Turkey Creek and Minnehaha Flat. Jackson McCracken, like Taylor, had also been a member of the Walker Party, and was part of the First Territorial Legislature. He was apparently notorious for his lack of personal hygiene, and his fellow legislators refused to allow him to take his seat until he bathed and groomed himself. He refused, so they took him to Granite Creek and forcibly bathed him and cut his beard and hair. He later went on to discover the fabulous McCracken Mine and eventually retired to a beautiful ranch in the Santa Cruz Mountains of California, which became, according to Farish, "...a place of resort for men like Ambrose Bierce, Bret Harte and others..."9 Jim Fine was to become one of the major pack train operators in the Bradshaws.

By August, 1870, there were two arrastras at work at the Del Pasco. On August 15, McCracken, Taylor, Hogle and Fine returned to Prescott with 112 ounces of gold at $17 to the ounce, or $1,904 worth. This was a yield of $300 per ton, and the vein was becoming richer and thicker. Now the *Miner* really warmed up: "...for our miners have found a great thing, a big thing. This 'thing' is not more nor less that the richest gold mine in the world, which had been named the 'Del Pasco' and is situated upon the summit of the Bradshaw Mountain, about thirty miles southeast from Prescott."10 By September there was a growing community of miners in the Bradshaws. A Mr. Christie located the New Era mine on a vein in a basin about a mile and a half from the Del Pasco. This is probably the first mention of Bradshaw Basin, the present site of Crown King. His partner was Mr. Poland, who gave his name to one of the major drainages in the area.

Hogle sold his interest in the Del Pasco to the Jackson brothers for $1,000 cash. The Jacksons then purchased a four-stamp mill, and hired S. C. Miller to haul it to the Bradshaw district. In the meantime, McCracken and Taylor had brought in another 116 ounces of Del Pasco ore from a run of twenty tons of crushed ore. By November, there were several new lodes in the Bradshaws including the Hidden Treasure, Star, Blandina, Oceanica and Belfast lodes, and several parties were preparing to spend the winter in the mountains. The Jackson's mill had been transported as far as Oak Creek before it was left for the winter. The only access to the area at this time was provided by a few primitive trails. By December, the Del Pasco was being timbered, and there were thirty experienced miners in the district. By March, 1871, the Prescott paper reported that every gulch near the Del Pasco was filled with placer miners who were making from five to twenty dollars a day with rockers and pans.

The Jackson brother's mill finally arrived at the Del Pasco and was fully operational by September, but lack of sufficient water prevented it from operating at full capacity. Water was expected to become more abundant as the rainy season progressed. In October, the Jacksons ran the mill for seventy-two hours and netted $700 to $800 worth of gold dust. By the end of 1871, they had struck a vein of water that allowed them to run the mill on a more regular basis, but at the same time they needed more dies and were unable to operate. By February, 1872, they had solved their problems and were running the mill for ten hours a day, turning out forty to fifty ounces of gold every few days. T. Brooks was the supervisor of a crew of five or six men. In April, Jesse Jackson brought seven pounds of Del Pasco gold to Prescott that was worth $1,400 from a ninety-six hour run of the mill, and not long after that they got $1,500 worth from a three day run. Work slowed temporarily when four oxen were stolen by Indians.

Reconstruction of a five-stamp mill, on display in Nevada City, California. A large cam, powered usually by animal or water power, alternately raised each stamp so it could then fall on and crush the ore.

Nearby, in War Eagle Gulch, one of the Jacksons and a man named Shupe had a tunnel over twenty feet long, and prospects looked good for a rich mine. By January, 1873, the Del Pasco mill was running on ore from the War Eagle Mine. In March, Jesse Jackson worked about thirty tons of War Eagle ore at the mill and produced $1,000 worth of concentrate. In May, it was reported that a well had been established at the Del Pasco so the mill could be run constantly, but by August it was shut down again due to lack of water. Jesse Jackson eventually resorted to recycling the water so he could run the mill nine hours a day.

By late 1873, there was a great deal of activity on the War Eagle lode. Goodwin and McKinnon, grubstaked by merchants in Wickenburg, were operating two arrastras, and had recovered $1,200 worth of concentrate. William Cole and a partner had sunk a sixty-foot shaft and developed a seventy-foot tunnel, and by early 1874, Jesse Jackson had a crew of seven working at the War Eagle. In August, 1874, Levi Bashford, a prominent Prescott businessman, bought 250 feet of the original Del Pasco, 250 feet of the original War Eagle and three-fourths of the Del Pasco mill, which by that time was crushing four and one-half tons of ore per day with a yield of about $150. Shortly after that, Solomon and Jesse Jackson sold their interests in the War Eagle Mine and Del Pasco mill to Cal Jackson and W. J. Tompkins. In 1878, Tompkins received patents to the discovery claim and first extension of the War Eagle lode.

By the early 1880s, mining interest had shifted to the Tiger, Peck and other mines in the area. The Del Pasco was worked only sporadically. A Mr. Godfrey, who had became manager of the property, was taking ore out of the old mine, and running the mill in 1879 and 1880. After this, there was little activity at the Del Pasco until 1884, when Robert Grigsby leased the mill and began shipping gold to Prescott. He apparently mined the Pine Tree lode rather than the Del Pasco. His reopening of the mill caused other miners to begin working in the Del Pasco area, but this burst of activity was short-lived.

Chapter Four:
The Initial Tiger Excitement

In late 1870, a few months after the discovery of the Del Pasco, there were reports of a few prospectors exploring in the far southern end of the Bradshaws. In December, 1870, Hod Curry and Dud Moreland reported that they had dug a thirty-foot shaft on a lode with two and a half feet of rich ore. In January, 1871, Hammond and Head reported a rich silver ledge in the area, but it was not until February that the magnitude of the strike was realized. Dud Moreland returned to Prescott with 500 pounds of ore which assayed at from 800 to 1500 ounces of silver per ton from what he called the Tiger Mine. The lode was reported to be seen for three miles at a width of six feet. The news caused tremendous excitement in Prescott, and a rush began that was compared to the Comstock strike in Nevada. Within a few days there were a hundred men in the area, and the *Miner* feared that it would lose all of its employees. The paper reported that a town site was located by Postmaster Bernard and others, "...on a high, level mesa, overlooking the large creek which washes the southwest foot of the Bradshaw range."11 This was probably the site of Moreland City, which was on a flat just below the Tiger Mine. The Tiger itself was perched on a steep, chaparral-clad slope on the southwest edge of the Bradshaws. The county recorder was said to be extremely busy recording deeds and claims, and Prescott itself appeared deserted as everyone headed for the Bradshaws. Mr. Riggs, a Nevada silver miner, reported that the Tiger was far richer that the Comstock, but there were also reports of conflicts and claim jumpers, and there was fear that blood would be shed.

Claims at the Tiger were two hundred feet long, and they were being sold for no less than thirty to fifty dollars per foot. The previous high had been fifteen dollars per foot. Ore was to be shipped to San Francisco and Virginia City for assay and inspection. By March, claim footage in the Tiger and the neighboring Eclipse Mine were going for one hundred dollars per foot, and parties were constantly leaving Prescott for the district. A pack train was established by Mr. Simmons to haul ore to Prescott, and several other mines were established in the area, including the Eclipse, Gray Eagle, Clipper, Cougar and Rhinoceros. By mid-March, there were said to be 150 men in the Bradshaws, and forty men were building a road to the area. An assay office had been opened, and several houses were being built.

In spite of this sudden influx of white men into the mountains, Indians were still a threat. A Colonel Snivelly and six other men were looking for a route for a road from the Bradshaws to Phoenix when they were attacked. Snivelly and three others were killed and their bodies mutilated.

Incidents such as these, however, did not discourage the miners and merchants. A. E. Davis turned several wagons of merchandise back from Williamson Valley towards the Bradshaws, where he planned to open a store. The only wagon route at the time was through Skull Valley and Walnut Grove. The road ended at Minnehaha Flat, and trails were being opened from there into the mountains. In April, 1871, the town site of Bradshaw City, which was to become the "capitol" of the Bradshaws for many years, was laid out. According to the Prescott *Miner:* "Mr. Case, Deputy U.S. Surveyor, has been engaged in laying out a town site on top of Bradshaw Mountain. The location is a beautiful one, on the south-west side of the 'basin', a little north of the divide, above Poland's cabin, in the midst of a fine growth of pine timber, and with a plentiful supply of the purest water from large springs which bubble out of the everlasting granite. The location is held by eight persons, there being ten shares in the company, ... and the point is well chosen and central, being at the junction of the trails from Prescott, via the Del Pasco mine to the Tiger and the Eclipse, and from Minnehaha Flat, via the mountain trail, to the same place."12 Town lots were 25x120 feet, and several log buildings were completed or under construction. Two stores run by Davis and Shekels, and Collier and Beardslee, were operating, and H. Hagen was about to open a restaurant. A saloon and

Noah Shekels, early owner of general stores at Bradshaw City and the Tiger Mine. Later, he was a partner in the Crowned King Mine.
Courtesy Sharlot Hall Museum

assay office were also under construction, and a well was being dug.

In May, 1871, the Tiger Mining District was established, and its laws were printed in the *Weekly Arizona Miner*. By this time, there were three hundred miners in the Bradshaws, and an advertisement for the Silver Summit Hotel and Store appeared in the Prescott paper. A Bradshaw Town Association was set up with W. C. Collier as president. The town site was one mile square. Another big event in May, 1871, was the first visit of a woman to the district. She was Mrs. Charles A. Luke of Prescott, and she was presented with a two pound silver brick. Her husband, a prominent

member of the famous Luke family of Arizona, was mayor of Prescott, and would later become heavily involved in mining in the Bradshaws.

That same month the *Miner* reported that: "At Bradshaw City, everything is lively, a crowd of men is cutting timber, teams are hauling logs, building is brisk, and everybody sanguine. Dr. N. Beardslee hauled 1,200 pounds of merchandise over the new road from Minnehaha Flat to his store, last week."13 A restaurant, the Nevada, was established by Chandler and Hagan. In June, the Fashion saloon, run by Gordon and Wilkerson, was opened. T. Garrison started to advertise his express line, and J. A. Simpson ran a saddle train from Prescott to the Bradshaws. Eight hundred dollars was raised to improve the trail from Prescott to the new district. Another town, called Marion, was to be established at Minnehaha Flat to catch the traffic en route to the mountains.

In July, the first reported incidence of violence occurred in Bradshaw City. L. S. Wainwright shot and killed R. Landsdon in a squabble over a house and lot. An innocent bystander was also hit by a stray bullet and was not expected to survive. Wainwright was arrested by constable Gregory and brought to Prescott, where he was released on $3,000 bail.

Building continued in the area, as housing was erected in Bradshaw City, Moreland City, and Marion. A dairy was operating near Bradshaw City, and another was to start near Marion. In July, Bradshaw City's second saloon, the Progressive, was advertising. The first sermon in the Bradshaws was delivered by Parson Groves on Sunday July 9, 1871. Arizona Governor Safford visited the district and proclaimed the Tiger richer than the Comstock.

In spite of the large number of miners in the mountains, Indians continued to be a problem. A party led by Jackson McCracken, that was heading down Black Canyon, was surrounded by Indians and had to beat a hasty retreat. Indians had also stolen two horses from the Eclipse camp, and had attempted to steal a herd of cattle while dressed as white men. A rancheria, or campsite, had been found fifteen miles north of Bradshaw and an attack was planned. In early 1872, Indians stole livestock at Bradshaw City, and four work oxen at the Del Pasco mill. The Tiger Mining Company was unable to ship ore because Indians had stolen their mules. Dud Moreland chased off eight Indians who were trying to steal his cattle; he killed one and wounded two others.

The Tiger Silver Mining Company was incorporated in San Francisco on July 20, 1871, with capital of $2,400,000. The *Los Angeles Times* reported that Tiger ore, with an average value of $1,028 per ton, had been shipped through Los Angeles. The company had sixteen men working in two shafts, one down one hundred feet, and the other down eighty to ninety feet. Several prominent Prescott businessmen, such as Levi Bashford, were involved in buying and selling "feet" in the Tiger and other mines, paying from $1,500 to $2,000 for one hundred feet.

In November, 1871, the *Miner* reported the first serious mining accident in the Bradshaws. A miner named "French Tom" fell ninety feet down the Tiger shaft, breaking through a platform of two-inch thick boards at the eighty-foot level. He regained consciousness, but was in agony and not expected to live. He died on October 14, 1871.

Most of the mines in the Bradshaws, except for the Tiger and the Del Pasco, shut down during the winter of 1871-72. The Tiger shaft was down to 180 feet by February, 1872. Mines all over the west were being named Tiger, in hopes that some of the Bradshaw mine's glory would rub off. In mid-1872, an offer of $150,000 was made to the Tiger's owners, but they refused to sell. Also at this time, the Mining Law of 1872 was passed, and O. H. Case surveyed the Tiger so that its owners could patent it under the new law. In early 1873, several Notices of Application for Patent for claims on the Tiger lode appeared in the *Weekly Miner*. Applicants included William Lent, Levi Bashford, C. C. Bean and

John Taylor. A great deal of rich ore remained on the Tiger dump, and the owners expected capital to be invested as soon as patents were obtained. Heavy rains in the summer of 1873 allowed the mills to run full time, although floods were a problem.

The Tiger was inactive during the winter of 1873-74, and the only inhabitants of the camp were Dud Moreland and George Hammond. They abandoned the camp for a seventeen-day prospecting expedition, and when they returned, they found that Indians had ransacked it. The Indians had stolen knives and clothes, and had vandalized the cabins. Hammond and Moreland hoped to persuade a cavalry patrol to search for the Indians, who, they believed, were somewhere between Humbug and Castle Creeks.

The patent for the original Tiger Mine was recorded on April 30, 1874. This was the first mine patented and recorded in Yavapai County. However, for the following three years there was little activity at the mine. There was some excitement in July of 1874, when the first mail arrived at Bradshaw City from Wickenburg. A regular mail route was established by early 1875, with Mr. Ferris as carrier. The route went from Wickenburg to Walnut Grove, then to Bradshaw and the Bully Bueno, and finally to the Quartz Mountain mill. A privately funded road had been started from Prescott to Bradshaw in late 1874. Expenses were to have been $2,500, and work began with six men, but eventually the work was halted by snow. Attempts were made to collect unpaid subscriptions so that work could begin again in the spring. A Mr. Hodge reported in 1876 that the Tiger had lain idle for years except for the work that Messrs. Riggs and Hammond were doing on the south extension of the Tiger. In February, 1877, the Aztlan mill near Prescott was processing Tiger ore brought in by Dud Moreland. The original excitement at the Tiger was short-lived, but over the years many more attempts would be made to make the mine a profitable venture.

Chapter Five:
Bradshaw Basin and Charles A. Luke

While the Tiger was booming, there was a great deal of mining and milling activity in the Bradshaw City area, also known as Bradshaw Basin, or the Pine Grove Mining District. In the Wheeler Report of 1872, there was said to be a wagon road from Walnut Grove to Bradshaw City. Bradshaw City then contained about a dozen log houses and a store. The Bradshaw City Post Office was established on July 1, 1874, with Noah C. Shekels as postmaster. In 1875, Collier, Roach, Luke, and Safenberg were planning to erect a forty-foot water wheel in Bradshaw Basin to run six arrastras near the Belfast and Hunter claims. Charles A. Luke and company's water wheel was reported to be in successful operation by April, 1875. It was intended to provide the power for nine arrastras and several stamps. However, it was shut down in early 1876 because of defects, one being that the wheel threw water into the belting. It was expected to be back in operation shortly. Jim Fine and Dan Martin were working the Buckeye lode, which was near the future site of the Crowned King mine.

By late 1876, during the lull in activity at the Tiger, there were said to be twenty-five or thirty buildings in Bradshaw City, but all were vacant except the one occupied by Charles Kautz, the postmaster and Justice of the Peace. The most active person in the Basin during this period was C. A. Luke, who had been in the restaurant and liquor business in Prescott, as well as having been its mayor. He sold his property in Prescott in order to devote all his energies to mining and milling in the Bradshaws. When it became apparent that his water wheel was not going to provide reliable power for his mill, he went to San Francisco to buy a quartz mill. He returned on the stage from San Francisco in early 1877, having

purchased the Constantia stamp mill near Ehrenberg. He arranged to have his mill moved to the Bradshaws, and planned to build a road from Walnut Grove to his millsite. Luke hired forty men and had them build his mill, construct a road to the millsite, and work the Gretna Mine, that showed silver at $250 to $300 per ton. By April, 1877, his road was nearly completed, and his mill had gotten as far as Walnut Grove. By May, the road was done and the first part of the mill had arrived in the Basin. The road followed Pine Creek from Minnehaha up toward the divide overlooking Bradshaw Basin, and was in the general area of the current Wagoner Trail. The mill was a ten-stamp mill driven by a forty horsepower engine which had been set up near Yuma for eight years, but was idle for several of those years. It was accompanied by a smelting furnace and an assay office. The mill was expected to start crushing ore on July fourth, with the arrival of the smokestack. It did run for a short while but was shut down quickly, since the smokestack still had not arrived from Skull Valley.

Several problems clouded the excitement of the opening of the mill. Martin Soffenberg fell twenty-four feet from the mill's water tank and suffered severe internal injuries. The son of superintendent Pletz went to Prescott to fetch Dr. Day. Another problem was encountered when it was discovered that the ore contained sulphurets, and had to be roasted before milling. Luke had to order a roaster from San Francisco, causing another delay. All of his efforts were in vain, however, because the August 31 issue of the *Weekly Miner* contained a notice of a sheriff's sale of Luke's ten-stamp mill on Saturday, September 15, at the Court House in Prescott. Luke was reported to be in San Francisco in early September, apparently trying to save his mill.

The final blow came in mid-September when the mill was flooded during heavy rains. Some damage was done, and there were two inches of water on the floor. The *Weekly Miner* of November 9, 1877, reported that Luke's mill had been sold at a sheriff's sale for $5,647.50 to satisfy a San Francisco investor. In February, 1878, the property of C. A. Luke, including his Montezuma building on Montezuma street in Prescott, was sold to satisfy his creditors. Luke's attempt to establish himself in the Bradshaws had failed.

Luke's mill, later to become known simply as the Basin Mill, and finally to be expanded into the Crowned King Mine's mill. Luke had it moved from near Yuma to Bradshaw Basin in 1877. Courtesy Prescott National Forest

Chapter Six:
The Tiger Again

Tiger, or Moreland City, as seen from the west.
The mine is just out of sight to the left.
Courtesy Sharlot Hall Museum

One event that greatly increased the possibility of successful mining in the Bradshaws was the removal of the Apache Indians from Yavapai County. In February, 1875, 1,476 Apaches were moved from the Verde Valley to the San Carlos Reservation by fifteen soldiers and forty Indian allies. One of the main deterrents to investment in the area's mines had been the fear that Indians would impede progress, or stop a mine from producing altogether. This threat no longer existed.

The architect of the next attempt to make the Tiger a paying mine was J. H. Helm. In July, 1877, he bonded the mine for six months, and was obligated to do $10,000 worth of work there. After six months, he was either to pay the owners two dollars per share of stock, or return the mine to the owners with any ore he had removed. Mr. Helm was obviously a strong believer in the future of the Tiger, and was not afraid to gamble on it. In August, Pell Craigue, who was operating the mine for Helm, reported that a road had been completed from the Tiger to Luke's road, and that hoisting works and pumps were being hauled from Ehrenberg. The mine was to be completely overhauled, and expectations were high that it would once again be a big ore producer. Ex-governor Safford scheduled a visit to the rejuvenated mine.

In February, 1878, a rich body of ore was found at the Tiger. It was said to be twenty feet wide, with ore worth up to $4,000 per ton. Specimens of ore brought to Prescott ran as high as $15,000 per ton. The new Tiger Mining Company was incorporated with J. D. Fry as president. Directors included George Bowers, Levi Bashford and E. O. F. Hastings.

One hundred thousand shares were issued at one hundred dollars each. J. H. Helm was to be the general superintendent.

The rebirth of the Tiger stimulated the economy of the entire area. George Hammond opened a saloon to serve the Tiger, and there were plans for mills at the Tiger and two neighboring mines, the Gray Eagle and the Oro Bonito. The California owners of the Oro Bonito authorized a road contract to connect their mine with Bradshaw City, since their mill was being shipped from California. The Oro Bonito, later part of the Oro Bella group, was located in the canyon where Humbug Creek flows out of the Bradshaws, about a mile south of the Tiger. James Patterson was given the contract to construct the Oro Bonito road and deliver the mill. In the *Weekly Miner* of November 1, 1878, he advertised for twenty-five men to work for him. After hauling the Oro Bonito's mill, Patterson was hired by the Tiger to bring in their mill. There is a later account of this story, still told today, that maintains that Patterson was hired to haul the mill to the Oro Bonito, but since there was no road, the owners assumed that he would have to build one. Instead, he drove the wagons to the top of Wasson Peak, high above the mine, and then lowered the wagons and equipment down the steep slope. He had to abandon the wagons, but that was cheaper than building a road. Also at this time, to reflect the shift in activity in the area, the Bradshaw election precinct was moved from Bradshaw City to the Tiger Mine by the County Board of Supervisors.

The Tiger Mining Company was in the process of constructing new hoisting works along with a forty-by-ninety foot building to protect the men and machinery. C. H. Sturty was to take charge of the hoisting works, and a ten-stamp mill was on order from a firm in San Francisco. The mill was to be completed in ninety days. C. D. Genung was hired to haul the 30,000 pounds of hoisting equipment from Kirkland Valley to Walnut Grove. The mill was en route from Ehrenberg. A saw mill for

the mine had already arrived at Minnehaha Flat. In December, 1878, there were eighty-two men working at the Tiger Mine, about fifty working at the Oro Bonito, and another fifty at the mill in Bradshaw Basin. In mid-January, 1879, the Tiger mill arrived at Walnut Grove, pulled by five twelve-mule teams. The machinery was to be transferred to Patterson's ox-pulled wagons for the rest of the trip.

While the Tiger was said to be the liveliest camp in the Territory, there was not much happening at Bradshaw City. Apparently, the only people left in town were Judge Kautz, the Justice of the Peace, and Noah Shekels, the storekeeper. By April of 1879, Shekels had also moved to the Tiger, while his wife was expecting a baby. A petition was circulated to move the post office from Bradshaw City to the Tiger Mine, even though there had been no mail delivery to the area for months. Mr. and Mrs. Grove were now operating a boarding house at the Tiger. The Tiger's hoisting works were completed at this time and the mill was to be finished in six weeks. There were one hundred men working at the Tiger; some were working on the old shaft, some were sinking a new one, and others were putting up the mill. The mine was at the 400-foot level, and the mill was to be running by May 15. The new shaft was to go down 900 feet where a tunnel would cross seventy-five feet to the lead.

By April of 1879, the boom at the Tiger had spread to the whole area. Mail service was resumed to the Bradshaws, with the post office now located at Shekels' store at the Tiger. A first-class hotel was planned for the Tiger, and Sandy Hammond was building a saloon there. A brewery at the Tiger boasted the best beer in the Territory. Even Bradshaw City revived itself, and all of its houses were now rented. There was also a store, feed yard, restaurant and smithy in operation there.

The Tiger mill was officially started on June 9, 1879. Witnesses at this inaugural run included J. H. Helm, the superintendent; James Mee, representing the mill's builders; Levi Bashford and Mr. Allen, directors of the company, and Mrs. Groves and her daughter, of the Tiger Hotel. Mee was working at the Peck mine, and would later develop the Tuscumbia mine. The new mill had to be shut down after a short time because the roaster was becoming clogged with pulp, but it was running again in a couple of weeks. By July, the mill was turning out $2,000 worth of bullion per day. During that month, the Tiger shipped twenty-six bars of bullion to San Francisco, worth about $36,000. Clearly, the reopened Tiger was a big success.

Also during this period, school districts were opened at the Peck and Tiger mines with about thirty children. Helm, the Tiger superintendent, went home to California for a month to rest, according to the *Weekly Miner*, from "...overwork and over anxiety."[14]

The Tiger Mine, as it appeared in the 1880s looking from the west.
Courtesy Crown King Saloon

Chapter Seven:
Bradshaw Basin--1878 - 1881

A meeting was held on June 1, 1878, in the Bradshaw City Post Office by the miners of the Tiger and Pine Grove Mining Districts. Dud Moreland was elected chairman, and boundaries were agreed upon, since the districts were adjacent. Boundary descriptions for both districts began at Noah Shekels' house in Bradshaw City.

At roughly the same time, C. A. Luke's Bradshaw Basin stamp mill was purchased at a sheriff's sale by Curtis Coe Bean for the May Bean Mining Company. Bean had been one of the discoverers of the Peck Mine. The price mentioned was $5,801.25; disagreeing slightly from an earlier report that put the price at $5,647.50. The mill was to run ore from the Loreno, Cougar and Gray Eagle mines. Bean had also bought Hoefler's ten-stamp mill on Arrastra Creek near Walnut Grove, so he now owned thirty stamps in the Prescott area. By the winter of 1878, Bean had remodeled the mill, and was ready to run Gray Eagle ore, but was delayed because the snow was too deep to allow the ore to be packed in. However, legal problems were to cause him even more difficulties in early 1879. Although he had spent a great deal of money repairing the mill, Bean had apparently not satisfied all of the requirements after buying it at the sheriff's sale. The mill was, therefore, resold by the sheriff to an attorney representing a group of lien claimants against the mill. Bean maintained that the terms of the sale had been misrepresented and allowed the resale, rather than meet the unexpected obligations which apparently involved liens on the property that had been established when Luke had owned it. Bean, however, was determined to own the mill, and now tried a different tack. He purchased the Goldwater's interest in the mill, and obtained a Sheriff's deed. He then sued fifty-two defendants for

Curtis Coe Bean, owner of the Bradshaw Basin Mill, and a partner in the Peck Mine.
Courtesy Sharlot Hall Musuem

quiet title. In an irate letter to the *Weekly Miner*, he wrote, "I have at a cost of seven thousand dollars rebuilt the mill. I walked into a crazy, rickety mill, with the engine on rotten logs for a foundation, and the fly-wheel buried in mud. A battery that could not stand alone, and pulleys afflicted with delirium tremens, and I walked out leaving it one of the finest ten-stamp mills on the Pacific coast, and I did it legally."[15]

The most prominent inhabitants of Bradshaw City during this period were still Noah Shekels, who ran the general store and post office, and Judge Kautz, who had been there for eight years. A petition was circulated at this time to move the post office from Bradshaw City to the Tiger Mine, where there was more activity.

There was some excitement when a gang of counterfeiters was arrested in Bradshaw City by Deputy Sheriff Dodson. A. W. Hausborough and two accomplices were believed to be making bogus Mexican coins in Hausborough's cabin. The molds were found, but the suspects were released for lack of evidence as to who was actually the guilty party. The case was to be retried.

In the summer of 1879, a few men, led by W. C. Colyer and Theodore Loiston, demonstrated their faith in the future of Bradshaw City by grading streets and making new lots; but their optimism was unfounded, and the town never regained its earlier level of activity. In July, 1879, Judge Kautz died and Thomas Campbell was appointed as the new Bradshaw Justice of the Peace.

The Bradshaw Basin mill was working again, processing silver from the Black Warrior. The mill was operated at this timeby Bowen, Knowles and Company. They had erected a new water tank at the mill and were planning to work ore from the Tip Top Mine that was to be packed in. In May, 1880, a bar of silver bullion, worth about $1,200, was shipped from the Basin mill to Prescott. In July of 1880, a trial was still in progress to establish the rights of the lienholders against the Basin mill. In December, the Basin mill was leased for one year by Mrs. Mary Bean, to be operated by her agent and husband, C. C. Bean. Bean placed an advertisement in the *Weekly Miner* for the mill. Also at this time, the Bradshaw Basin Mill and Mining Company placed an attachment on the Silver Prince and Black Warrior mines, and sued their New York syndicate owners to recover the $6,000 they lost when the mines had not fulfillied their contract to supply ore to the mill. By March of 1881, the mill was processing Silver Prince and

Black Warrior ore under the direction of a Mr. Morton, who had apparently leased the mill from the Beans. Bill Simmons was bringing eighty mules in from Globe to pack ore to the mill.

However, another disagreement developed between the mine and mill operators. Four employees of the mill removed four or five thousand dollars worth of Prince and Warrior ore from the mill, and refused to return it until the mine owners paid them for their work. The mine owners refused to bargain when the mill workers doubled their demands, and, as a result, both the mines and mill were shut down for a time. It was next reported that the mill was operating in December of 1881.

In June, 1880, a fire destroyed several buildings in Bradshaw City. It originated in the post office, being operated by deputy postmaster Ira Woods. "The post office building, owned by J. J. Jonas, and another building, owned by W. R. Logan, together with the contents of saloon and furniture, were also consumed. Loss at present writing and cause of fire unknown. Great credit is due to the citizens for their prompt action in saving other building adjoining."[16] This was reported to the Prescott *Weekly Miner* by Justice of the Peace Tom Campbell.

In late July, 1880, the post office in Bradshaw City was discontinued. In the election of 1880, forty-five votes were cast in the combined Bradshaw and Tiger district. Travelers who passed through Bradshaw City in March, 1881, found, "...that of some twenty houses, some of which are capacious and well built, not one is inhabited. Desolation reigns supreme in the city of the Bradshaws."[17]

Chapter Eight: The Tiger 1879 - 1880--
Disaster and Disappointment

In August of 1879, a horrible mining accident occurred at the Tiger. The mine was running three shifts at the time. Each shift was lowered down the 350-foot-deep shaft in an immense tub attached to a wire cable. As reported in the *Weekly Miner*, the third shift was being lifted out for lunch at two o'clock in the morning, "...when within a hundred feet of the top coming up for lunch, the reel became unhitched, and the entire cable, which weighs 700 pounds, unwound, and men, tub and cable were all precipitated to the bottom of the shaft."18 The cable operator was Ike Patrick, and there were rumors that he had been drinking, although this was not reported by the newspaper. Charles Conkling and George Watson went down another shaft, and then crossed to the scene of the accident. "Watson says the scene was horrible beyond description. McAuliffe lay under the bucket, the edge of it and part of the cable over him, and McDonald, whose neck was broken, across him. . . . Reese was partly under McA., but more in the corner, so that the full weight was not on him, he is bruised and sore from the fall but has not a bone broken, and is not seriously injured. Hickey was next, lying to one side with his right leg shattered below the knee and badly cut in the skull, but conscious. Sullivan lay across the tub, bent backwards with nearly all

The Bradshaw City cemetery when the wooden grave markers were still in place.
They have long since been destroyed. Courtesy Prescott National Forest

the cable on his body, his skull smashed dreadfully; he had apparently struck the wall. He lived two hours but was totally unconscious.

"Jack Sullivan and Jack McDonald, being dead, were laid out at the hoisting works... A black flag was hoisted, work was stopped, stores and saloons closed, and the comrades of the dead men put on black badges. Six of their friends dug the graves, two more made the coffins, covering them with black lining and cushioning them very nicely.

"The Episcopal funeral service was read by Mr. Green. Teams from Bradshaw came over for hearses, and at half-past two, the entire camp formed in procession and marched to Bradshaw Basin, where the remains of the poor unfortunate men were laid to rest under the waving pines. One hundred and twenty people attended the funeral, being the entire population except the wounded and their nurses."19 These were the first burials in the Bradshaw City cemetery, which can still be found in a high saddle between the Tiger Mine and the site of Bradshaw City.

McAuliffe died later that day and was also buried in the cemetery. Reese recovered, but Hickey was sent to Prescott to have his leg amputated. Hickey later sued the Tiger company for $50,000. While rushing to the scene of the accident from Prescott, the ambulance in which Dr. Ainsworth was riding was upset near Turkey Creek, and the messenger who had come for the doctor broke his leg. The doctor was delayed while helping this man, who was taken to Alexandra. The Tiger incident was said to be the worst mining accident in Arizona to date, and the *Weekly Miner* closed its story on the funeral by saying that: "This is now the saddest and quietest camp in the mountains."20

Other, less serious, inconveniences and problems plagued the Tiger company. In September, in spite of the shortage of water, someone put soap in two of the wells, rendering them useless for days. Freighters hauling 100,000 pounds of salt to the mine, used in the processing of ore, took over two months to

travel the twenty-eight miles from Walnut Grove to the Bradshaws. Dud Moreland, one of the Tiger's first discoverers, brought suit against the company for the recovery of his original discovery claim. The Tiger also lost its school at this time when Miss Augie Miller moved her school from there to Walnut Grove. Finally, Hickey was awarded $10,000 in his suit against the Tiger, although the company planned to appeal.

Another serious mining accident capped off this string of bad luck. A blasting accident killed William Mozart, and wounded David Fellows and Matt Carr. They had drilled five holes, filled them with charges and set them off, but one had failed to detonate. When they returned to clear away the rock, one of the miners struck the unexploded cap and set it off. Dr. Ainsworth again came to aid the wounded, but Fellows died while Ainsworth was taking him back to Prescott. Mozart had quit working at the Vulture mine near Wickenburg because he considered it an unsafe mine.

Another accident involved the mine's chief engineer, who wounded his hand and died of lockjaw. His name was McPherson, and he was also buried in the Bradshaw City cemetery.

However, in spite of all these difficulties, the Tiger continued to prosper. In October, 1879, the mine shipped $29,000 worth of ore. The Tiger company was planning to reorganize and incorporate in New York, paying dividends of twenty-five cents per share. They also hoped to increase the mill capacity by twenty stamps. The president of the Tiger Mining Company was now ex-governor R. C. McCormick, whose offices were in New York City. The mine now employed fifty men, who were paid three to six dollars per day. During December, the Tiger mill shipped nearly $40,000 in silver bars to San Francisco. The gross annual yield of the Tiger was estimated at over one-half million dollars. That would result in $350,000 in clear profit.

There was also a hospital at the Tiger,

30

established by Dr. Day of Prescott, as well as a mercantile company owned by E. J. Bennett and F. M. De Bord.

In spite of these good times, a scandal concerning financial mismanagement seemed to sour confidence in the Tiger. Some of the Tiger checks, drawn on a San Francisco establishment, turned out to be bad. Prescott businessman F. W. Blake levied an attachment on the property of the company to secure payment for bad checks worth about $2,000. This attachment so incensed Tiger superintendent Helm that he shut down the mine and mill, and discharged the men. A telegram soon arrived from San Francisco, authorizing the Arizona Bank to honor all Tiger checks. However, Helm never returned to work, and the company sent another superintendent from San Francisco.

In July, 1880, the Tiger Mining Co. changed its name to the Tiger Mill and Mining Co., with stock to be exchanged share for share. McCormick was still president, with C. B. Foster in charge of the property. In August, 1880, Charles Wurth closed his brewery business at the Tiger, a sure sign that things were not going well. Ex-governor Safford visited the mine in September, and it was hoped that his visit would cause work to be started again. In the election of 1880, there were about forty-five voters in the Tiger and Bradshaw area, but later that month it was reported that the mine was quiet, with few people working there. This second Tiger boom seemed to have been ended by a few bad checks and a temperamental superintendent.

Tiger, or Moreland City, looking west. The photograph was taken from the mine itself. Courtesy Crown King Saloon

Edmund George Peck first came to Arizona from New Mexico in 1863 with W. G. Collier and others, after word of the Walker party discoveries had reached Santa Fe. In 1864, he was in command of a squad of twenty men in King Woolsey's second expedition against the Apaches, when one hundred well-armed men killed about thirty Indians. He was said to be a crack shot. He was an Army scout from 1867 to 1871 working for General Frank Wheaton at Fort Whipple. He also had the first hay contract at Fort Whipple, which was then in Chino Valley.

Edmund "Ed" G. Peck
Courtesy Sharlot Hall Museum

Peck first visited the future mine site with Dan O'Leary, but Peck was prevented from examining the minerals by O'Leary, who said he wouldn't be found guilty of owning a mine in so rough and uncivilized a country. It is elsewhere reported that Peck had first seen the rich quartz ledge near War Eagle Creek while scouting for the military, but seeing little gold in it, he ignored it. He was later shown a sample of silver ore and realized that it was similar to what he had seen in War Eagle Gulch. He returned to the site in the summer of 1875 with Curtis Coe Bean, William Cole and Thomas M. Alexander, and they rediscovered the ledge. They returned to Prescott with 100 pounds of ore that assayed in the thousands of dollars. The first ten tons of Peck ore were sold for $13,000. Bean was listed in the 1870 census as a thirty-nine year old broker from New Hampshire. He had been a candidate for Congress the previous year, but was defeated. Thomas Alexander was Peck's father-in-law. William Cole had worked the War Eagle lode in the same area in 1873.

The Peck lode consisted of three parallel ledges, projecting as much as twenty feet above the surface. The original work was on the south ledge where the vein was about two feet wide. The ore was so rich that miners feared that it could not last.

Transportation was, as with all Bradshaw mines, a huge expense. It cost the Peck about $80 per ton to ship the ore to San Francisco where it could be processed. It cost $40 just to pack the ore to Prescott, $30 from Prescott to Ehrenberg and $10 from Ehrenberg to San Francisco. By August of 1875, there were seven men working at the Peck, and forty miners in the vicinity. Ed Peck was building a house for himself and his family, and planned to spend the rest of his life there. The Peck partners had also developed the Occident Mine on the ledge parallel to the original Peck. Miners speculated that the belt of silver stretched from the Tiger group on the south to near Big Bug Creek several miles to the north. Two other major mines in the area were the

Silver Prince and its extension, the Black Warrior. South extensions of the Silver Prince extended for over 20,000 feet into Bradshaw Basin, and ended at the Old Dominion.

By November, the Peck company was erecting a smelter at the mine, and there was mail service once a week on the route between Wickenburg and Prescott. A boarding house, run by Mr. and Mrs. McMillan, was opened, and Jim Fine, who was packing ore for the Peck, had also opened a tent saloon and was hauling lumber from Bradshaw City with which to build a wooden saloon. By March of 1876, the shaft descended 160 feet, with the best ore assaying at $12,000 per ton. They removed $6,000 to $7,000 worth of ore daily. The town of Alexandra was laid out up the canyon from the Peck, and buildings were erected. The town was named for T. M. Alexander's wife by feminizing it to Alexandra. Peck and Fine leased lots in Alexandra for $100 each. Colonel Bigelow was in charge of laying out the town, selling lots and grading streets. The Peck company did not allow building on the Peck itself because they needed the land for their own use. Bean, in the meantime, was busy in San Francisco, trying to buy a mill for the new mine.

A meeting of leading citizens was held in Prescott to discuss ways and means of building a road to the Peck and Bradshaw area. Wells, the district attorney, felt that it would not be possible to raise enough money through taxation, so a committee was appointed to explore other methods. Ed Peck and George Opdyke were appointed to explore routes for the road.

In May of 1876, Governor Safford accompanied Ed Peck and C. C. Bean to the Bradshaws to look at the Peck and other mines in the area. The actual work at the Peck was being done under contract by Colonel Bigelow.

In June of 1876, an event occurred that would sour the relationship among the owners of the Peck, and create legal problems that were to have repercussions for years. William Cole, one of the Peck's original discoverers,

went on a drinking and spending spree that included his "...deeding away portions of his interest to lewd women of the town..."[21] He was drunk for an extended period, and the other Peck owners attempted to have him arrested. An acquaintance of Cole's recalled that Cole claimed to have a tapeworm and "...the worm eternally wanted whiskey..."[22] When he finally sobered up, he signed over his remaining interest in the mine to Mary Bean, wife of C. C. Bean. A month later, he regretted this action and brought suit against Bean and his wife, charging that they had conspired to debauch and extort him to sign over his interest in the Peck and Occident while he was drunk. The Beans responded that the deed had been a legal conveyance, and that Mary Bean had assumed the considerable debts incurred by Cole while he was on his spree. Judge Tweed ruled that Cole had no case, but that the deed was only a mortgage for payment of the indebtedness of Cole to the partnership. This did not satisfy the Beans.

"It was funny during the Cole-Bean trial to see with what earnestness and industry the friends of the plaintiff, Cole, labored to make him out the most worthless, contemptible, despicable, vile, miserable, pitiful, trifling, foolish, low-lived creature on earth, while his enemies were equally intent on exalting him to a comparatively respectable position..."[21] Apparently Cole's friends succeeded in destroying his name, and the local paper suggested that no one would consider him a catch for their daughter, in spite of the fact that the deed was only a mortgage, and Cole still had an interest in one of the richest mines in the territory.

By September, 1876, Alexandra contained twenty buildings and there were sixty men working mines in the area. The Peck's main shaft descended 230 feet and the main tunnel was 275 feet long, with ore running from $1,000 to $3,000 per ton. Along with all of this success, a few mishaps befell the prospering citizens. Colonel Bigelow borrowed a mule from Andy Shrope and rode it from

33

Prescott to Alexandra, but when he mounted it for the return trip the mule bucked him off and then chased and "...kicked him all over the town site and out into the suburbs."24 He finally retrieved the mule and rode it to Prescott in record time.   Another misfortune occurred during a lunch stop on a trip from the Peck to Prescott, when C. C. Bean was accidentally shot in the knee by a pistol that discharged inside a saddlebag that had been thrown on the ground. Finally, Jim Fine, local packer and saloonkeeper, was charged with shooting into a crowd at the Peck. More general misfortune occurred when mail service to the Bradshaws was stopped, in spite of the growing population.

On December 9, 1876, the Peck Mining Company filed articles of incorporation with 100,000 shares at $10 each. In the same time period, the Peck sent $3,500 worth of silver ore to be processed at the Aztlan mill near Prescott. The Peck Company was now constructing a road from the mine to the timber on Del Pasco ridge. The mine itself descended 220 feet, and the operators were hoisting one to two thousand gallons of water out of the shaft every twenty-four hours. The vein was still three feet wide and paying over $400 per ton. In February of 1877, the miners found a pocket of ore valued at $10,000 to the ton. The owners of the Peck purchased the Aztlan mill in Prescott in March, 1877, and in its first month under their ownership, the mill turned out $42,297.64 worth of bullion from Peck ore.

By early 1877, there were seventy-five people in Alexandra with two hotels, two saloons and a supply store. T. M. Alexander owned the store, Alexander McPhee was the constable, and Dave Grey was elected to bring mail to the town in lieu of postal service. The main street in Alexandra was called Prince Street, and there was much building going on.

There were plans to sell the mine for $400,000 in the spring of 1877, but when the sale fell through, the company decided to expand rather than sell. They purchased a mill to be put up near the mine, and planned to

Thomas M. Alexander, one of the partners in the Peck Mine.
Courtesy Sharlot Hall Museum

boost production from $60,000 to $200,000 worth of ore per month. By summer, there were forty men working at the Peck alone, and Alexandra had two stores, three boarding houses, four saloons, two livery stables, six houses, one butcher shop and a blacksmith shop, for a total of nineteen buildings. The Peck had spawned a boom town.

It had been reported in February of 1877 that the Black Warrior Mine had purchased a mill which was being shipped to the mine from San Francisco. Before the mill was set up at the Warrior, it was sold to the Murat company on Turkey Creek. It was then sold by the Murat company to the Peck company that summer, and hauled piecemeal from Ehrenberg to be set up in War Eagle gulch at the Peck. It was a ten-stamp mill with an attached furnace to pre-treat the ore, and it included a saw mill. James Patterson was hired to haul the mill from the Agua Fria, and built a road from Wolf Creek to the Peck.

During that same summer of 1877, mail service was restored to the Bradshaws, and a contract to complete a road from Prescott to the

Bradshaws was awarded to the lowest bidder. The contract, worth $32,000, was awarded to the same James Patterson who was hauling the mill to the Peck. Most of the road work was required between Prescott and Battle Flat. The Peck company itself was already building a road from War Eagle Gulch down Bear Creek, and had completed a lumber road up to the Del Pasco area. It was believed that at this time between three and four hundred people were buying their supplies at Alexandra.

There were several other signs of the incredible prosperity being experienced at the Peck. In September of 1877, a particularly rich sample of ore from the north tunnel of the Peck was assayed at $17,695.05 to the ton. The Peck crews were paid on Sunday nights in Alexandra, and sleep was impossible as pistol shots and shouts filled the air for most of the night. The Peck was now employing over one hundred and fifty people, and shipping $50,000 worth of ore per month. The improved road from Prescott to the Peck was finished at this time, and Ed Peck and C. C. Bean took the first coach ride to Alexandra. Finally, the Peck company was incorporated in San Francisco with capital stock of ten million dollars, and shares valued at one hundred dollars each.

The frame for the new Peck mill was being built under the supervision of James Mee. Mill machinery began arriving at the mine in October of 1877. The mill was to cost about $75,000, but at this time the Peck was producing $50,000 worth of ore per month, and milling the ore at the site would save a lot of money in freight costs. The Peck's payroll on November 1 was over $10,000.

In the midst of all this prosperity, legal problems began to rear their ugly heads once again. A decision in the Cole-Bean case had finally been reached, and Mary Bean's deed was declared void, since Cole was found to have been too drunk to conduct business intelligently. There were now two Peck companies: the original Arizona company headed by C. C. Bean, and the newly organized Cali-fornia Peck, under Ed Peck. Bean's Arizona company sued Peck's California company charging that it had failed to transfer ownership of the milling and mining properties to the Arizona company in exchange for one hundred thousand shares of capital stock as agreed. Bean's attorney asked that the California company be enjoined from taking possession of the property, which Peck was on his way to do.

The Arizona company held a meeting of the Trustees, which Peck and his father-in-law, T. M. Alexander, failed to attend. The company then packed the Trustees by adding new members and voting against Peck, affirming the Arizona company's action. They removed George Hogle as superintendent and replaced him with James Mee. Hogle was ordered to turn all bullion over to Bean, but when Bean went to the Aztlan mill to claim it, he found that Peck had already removed it. Bean's company then got an attachment on the $10,000 worth of bullion which was in the Wells Fargo safe. Sheriff Bowers called on the Wells Fargo agent, F. W. Blake, to turn over the bullion, which he did when Peck appeared and allowed the transfer to take place, under protest. The heart of the problem apparently was that some of the shares that were to have been transferred had been Cole's disputed holdings, to which Mary Bean lost ownership in the Cole-Bean case.

In the meantime, new directors were elected for the Peck Mining Company with Ed Peck as President. They expected that the California company would ultimately take over. However, this was delayed when Judge Tweed decided in favor of Mary Bean in her case against Peck, which prevented a takeover until after the case's final hearing. The Beans planned to take their case to the Supreme Court if necessary. James Mee, the mill superintendent, declared that if the company spent their money on mill supplies rather than legal fees, the mill would be running by then, and would have paid for itself in bullion.

Chapter Ten: The Black Warrior and Silver Prince

The Silver Prince Mine was discovered shortly after the Peck, and was on a vein adjacent to the Peck's. The Black Warrior was located as an extension of the Silver Prince. Both were later combined to become what is now known as the Swastika Mine, located high on the side of a ridge overlooking Crazy Basin, which is about halfway between Cleator and Crown King. It was the Black Warrior's mill that was eventually purchased by the Peck company and set up at that mine. In 1880, the owners of the Silver Prince Mine bought the Black Warrior and Tuscumbia mines. The new owners planned to build a new mill to serve all three mines. In the meantime, however, the Silver Prince company had their ore worked at the Bradshaw Basin mill. It was at this time that the dispute arose between the Prince and the men working at the mill. The mill workers refused to surrender the company's ore until they were paid. This disagreement led to the closing down of the Basin mill, and the Prince company made arrangements to have their ore worked at the Tuscumbia mill.

In 1882, there were twelve men working at the Black Warrior, extracting ore that yielded $2,000 per ton in silver. The superintendent was T. J. Eaman. Ore from the Black Warrior was shipped all the way to Omaha for treatment. Eventually, a mill was set up at the Black Warrior itself. By late 1883, the Warrior was working twenty-five men in the mine, and ten on the four-stamp mill. Ten thousand dollars worth of ore had been shipped to the owners in New York. In 1883, bullion output of the Black Warrior mill was estimated at $100,000. There is some disagreement among the sources as to whether the Black Warrior had a mill at the mine itself, or had its ore worked at the Tuscumbia mill. There are several contemporary newspaper reports of the operation of the Black Warrior mill, but Hamilton, in *The Resources of Arizona*, states that in 1884, the mine's ore was being worked at the Tuscumbia mill. Contemporary newspaper stories about the Tuscumbia mill reported that Eaman's company owned both the Black Warrior Mine and the Tuscumbia mill, and that the Warrior's ore was worked at the Tuscumbia.

In 1884, the Prince and Warrior company bought the Lane Mine, and packed ore from there to work it at the Warrior's mill.

In 1890, Steve Mott leased both the Black Warrior and Silver Prince, and he also purchased the Tuscumbia mill to work the ore from the various mines he was operating. He installed a steam hoist at the Prince, and in November, 1890, he was running the Tuscumbia mill twenty-four hours a day. However, when Ed Gobin leased the Prince in early 1891, several liens were filed against the mine because of money owed by Mott. In 1895, the mine was being worked by Sutherland and Cummins, and was said to be owned by New Yorkers.

Chapter Eleven: The Peck in 1878 and 1879-- More Legal Problems

Under the supervision of James Mee, the Peck mill was ready to start operations in January, 1878. Mee's contract called for him to start up the mill, run it for a while, and then turn it over to George Hogle, the superintendent. However, the mill would require eight to ten cords of wood a day, and there were only twenty-five cords on hand. Since there were no roads in the area, cut wood had to be hauled from nearby with small teams or sleds. To prepare for full operations, the company ordered 400 cords of wood for the mill.

The first run of the mill was successful, except that some inferior bricks used to build the roaster, or drying furnace, melted down and had to be replaced. Once this problem was remedied, the mill was operational, but still could only run about half the time because of the limited amount of water available. Once Mee had the Peck's mill running, he went to the Masterson mill, on Turkey Creek, to take charge. This mill was working ore from the Tuscumbia and Black Warrior mines at the time.

In spite of the successful operations at the Peck, the flurry of lawsuits continued unabated. The Peck company sued C. C. Bean for improperly spending $6,100 while he had been president. Bean then counter-sued the company for $4,280.26 that he claimed he had spent of his own money on the company's behalf while he had been running it. Mary Bean was suing the company for $494,000 for shares she claimed had been unlawfully seized by the company, and for shares that the company would not allow her to transfer or sell. Ed Peck was suing the Beans for conspiracy as a result of their seizing control of the Peck the previous year.

Meanwhile, the mine was still operating only twelve hours a day, and Alexander had discharged all the miners, leaving only enough men to work the mill. The mine was generating more ore than the mill could handle. Ed Peck made plans to lay pipe from the mine to the mill so that enough water could be supplied to run the mill full time. The mill superintendent was now a Mr. Hardy.

To further complicate the Peck's affairs, the Beans organized the May Bean Mining company, and attempted to take possession of the South Extension of the Peck. However, Bean's men were forced to abandon the claim when confronted by an armed crew from the Peck, led by Superintendent Hardy. The May Bean company then filed suit against the Peck company to prevent it from removing any property from the Aztlan mill. Charges had been filed against Hardy for driving off the Bean crew, but the charges were dismissed. Finally, Frank Schultz, the man who had led the Bean raid, sued the Beans for services rendered. Apparently, the lawyers of Prescott had no shortage of work.

The next round of the Peck battle involved the company's Aztlan mill in Prescott. In May, 1878, C. C. Bean took charge of the mill while the Peck company's guards were away. Bean and his men were then arrested for taking forcible possession of the mill, but were released on a writ of habeas corpus. There was an injunction on the mill, but the company continued to operate it with the proceeds held by a court-appointed receiver. Eventually, the charges against Bean were dismissed.

Finally, in June, Bean sold out to the Peck company for $50,000, plus the Peck's release of any claim on the Occident and South Extension of the Peck, and the Aztlan mill, which were claimed by the May Bean company. Bean then overhauled and reopened the Aztlan mill. This deal included the withdrawal

37

of all suits between the two parties so the Peck was finally able to concentrate on mining rather than litigation.

Through all of this, the Peck mine continued to prosper. In July, James Patterson completed a road from Prescott to Alexandra that cut ten miles off the old route. The mine was now producing about $2,000 per day, and was supporting twelve businesses in Alexandra, including several saloons and a brewery, a butcher shop, a dairy and four restaurants.

A rather bizarre incident occurred in September, 1878, when an employee of C. C. Bean's, Charles Blackburn, ran off with some of the May Bean company's bullion and another man's wife, leaving his own wife with a baby to support. Bean offered a reward for his capture. Blackburn and Mrs. Waite, the woman he had run off with, were captured in Prescott, but Blackburn escaped from jail when he was let out to consult with his lawyer. He

stole a horse from Judge Brooks, and a few days later stole a saddle from Bean's stable. He then rode into town at night, leading another stolen horse, presumably to rescue Mrs. Waite. As luck would have it, Blackburn passed Judge and Mrs. Brooks on the road, and Judge Brooks, recognizing his horse, grabbed it. Blackburn jumped onto the other horse and escaped, later abandoning the horse and stealing another horse and mule. To further complicate the scenario, he then kidnapped Mr. Waite, his lover's husband. They were later reported to be seen together along the Hassayampa, apparently on the best of terms. It was suspected that they were accomplices in some scheme rather than rivals for the same woman. They were both arrested in Walnut Grove by a deputy sheriff. Blackburn claimed to be insane. A couple of months later he tried to kill himself in jail by taking strychnine. He was eventually tried and found guilty, but

The Peck mill in operation. The rock outcropping that attracted Ed Peck's attention is in the background. Courtesy Sharlot Hall Museum

leniency was recommended. The local paper did not say what crime he had been found guilty of, or what his sentence was.

In the November elections of 1878, C. C. Bean was elected to the upper house of the Territorial Legislature. In this same period he also took a trip to San Francisco to buy a roaster for the Aztlan mill. Shortly thereafter, the May Bean Mining Company was incorporated with capital of $10,000,000. Bean was one of the directors. Bean was also planning another trip to San Francisco, Chicago, New York and Boston to convince capitalists to help develop Arizona's mines. He was obviously becoming one of the more important and influential men in the Territory.

F. W. Blake, a former Prescott mayor, was appointed as agent and general superintendent of the Peck Mining Company of Arizona in January, 1879. In April, Ed Peck, who had been in San Francisco, demanded that Blake turn over to him, as president of the company, the mine, mill and other property, and recognize his own man as superintendent. Blake, having been appointed by the Board of Trustees, refused to recognize Peck's authority. Peck then seized control of the mine with a band of armed men, and it looked as though a bloody confrontation was inevitable. However, Blake decided to proceed through the courts and the crisis was averted. The trial occurred in May, and the jury found in favor of the company, giving Ed Peck five days to yield possession of the mine through a court-appointed receiver, Judge Brooks. When Sheriff Walker went to the mine to take possession he was resisted by an armed force which claimed to be holding the mine under orders of Judge Porter of the Second District. The sheriff served his papers and returned to Prescott. Eventually, Judge Porter vacated his order and the company took over the mine, thus ending another chapter in the Peck mine follies.

Peck Canyon as it looks today. Courtesy Prescott National Forest

Chapter Twelve: Minnehaha Flat -- Gateway to the Bradshaws

During the early years of exploration and mining in the southern Bradshaws, the main route into the mountains was through Walnut Grove and Minnehaha Flat. Walnut Grove was a well-established community in its own right, but settlement in Minnehaha Flat came in response to traffic en route to Bradshaw City and the numerous mines at the south end of the Bradshaws, particularly the Tiger. In the early days, it was a picturesque flat containing grass and Ponderosa pines with Minnehaha Creek running through the center of it. Calvin Jackson was mentioned as the man who gave Minnehaha Flat its name.

The first known exploration of the Minnehaha area was by a group of prospectors led by Joseph C. Lennon. An eyewitness reported their journey. "While at work in a placer claim, in Big Bug district, in the summer of 1864 J. C. Lennon and other pioneers passed our camp rigged out for a 'prospect'. They rounded the Big Bug mountains and entered the Bradshaw range at or near the Minnehaha Flat, near which place they found and located a small, but rich gold ledge, which they named 'Minnehaha'. They worked the ore in an arrastra. It paid to do so. Indians were then troublesome and broke the 'party' all up. Before the break they found a great many more ledges and named the district 'Agua Fria'. In those days nobody thought of testing rock for silver, as gold was what people came there to 'dig'.

"The Lennon party's footsteps have since been trod by others. The once immense Agua Fria district is now divided into five or six districts embracing Tiger, Pine Grove, Silver Mountain, Lane, Humbug, Castle Creek and some others."[25] The 1864 Arizona census listed Joseph C. Lennon as a twenty-four year-old single miner from England.

The Wheeler expedition also passed through Minnehaha in 1872. "Following down this valley, along a wagon-road by a circuitous route we reached Minnehaha Flat, a densely-timbered plateau on the west slope of the Bradshaw Mountains."[26]

In 1871, trails were opened from the end of the wagon road in Minnehaha Flat to the mines and the newly developed settlement of Bradshaw City. Beardslee hauled 1,200 pounds of merchandise over the new road from Minnehaha to his new store in Bradshaw City. A town site named Marion was established in Minnehaha Flat, and a store was soon in operation with a sawmill, slaughter house and bakery under construction. A competing town named McCormick City was being established on Arrastra Creek. Charley Taylor, who had helped establish the Turkey Creek mining district in 1864, and had been one of the discoverers of the Del Pasco in 1870, established a farm on the Flat, and was to become a long-time citizen of the area. In 1874, Dud Moreland and Jim Fine reported that "...Charley Taylor's crops of corn and potatoes are the 'biggest thing in the mountains', and Charley would be happy if he only had a partner in calico."[27]

In 1878, James Patterson, the Bradshaw road builder, purchased the engine and boiler from the old Big Bug quartz mill, and the Peck Company's saw mill, in order to establish a saw mill in Minnehaha Flat. By early 1879, the saw mill was turning out 10,000 feet of lumber daily, and several houses were built in the area. Patterson was shipping lumber as far away as the famous Vulture Mine near Wickenburg. Minnehaha now had half a dozen families, and Charley Taylor had established a stage station. A post office was established on June 21, 1880, with Charley Taylor as postmaster. Charley thought that, because of the growth of the Mammoth Mine in the Silver Mountains, Minnehaha Flat would become the ". . . greatest mining camp on the Pacific Coast."28

James Patterson, keeping up his reputation as a road builder, constructed a road from Minnehaha Flat to Phoenix, through Oak Flat and Castle Creek. He was hauling lumber out and supplies in.

In the election of 1882, Charley Taylor was elected as a delegate to the Twelfth Legislative Assembly. In the same year, Charley lost his job as postmaster when the post office at Minnehaha Flat was discontinued and the mail went to Bradshaw. By 1885, Charley was, besides farming, also involved in mining. He had a fairly successful silver mine in Oak Flat, near Minnehaha.

An ambitious undertaking in Walnut Grove caused an increase in activity in Minnehaha Flat beginning in late 1886. A great dam was under construction across the Hassayampa River south of Walnut Grove. The dam, made mostly of rock fill, was to be

covered with a skin of pine boards. The pine boards were supplied by the saw mill at Minnehaha. The mill was no longer run by James Patterson, but rather by A. J. Head, who was apparently working exclusively for the Walnut Grove water storage company. A road was constructed from the dam to the saw mill, and more than three hundred thousand feet of lumber was delivered to the dam. By the summer of 1887, the dam was nearly finished and there was a sixty-foot deep lake that was a mile long and a half-mile wide. As the lake grew, Minnehaha Flat began to fill up with summer visitors from Phoenix, who came to enjoy the cool air and pine trees. Three years later, in February, 1890, the Walnut Grove dam burst after a heavy rain. The resulting flood killed fifty to sixty people, and was one of the worst disasters in Arizona history.

A large mining operation began near Minnehaha Flat in early 1888 at the Boaz Mine, between the Flat and the Silver Mountains. Apparently, the Boaz Mining Company was well financed, because in May of 1888,

The lake at Walnut Grove, looking south. The dam was in the notch, to the right of center, at the far side of the lake. Courtesy Prescott National Forest

Minnehaha Flat & the Boaz Mine

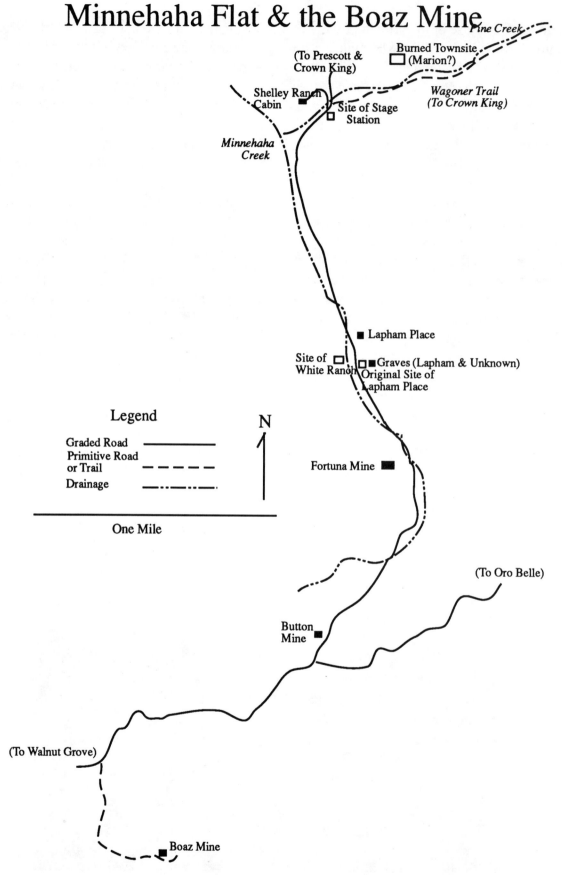

Pine Creek

Burned Townsite (Marion?)

(To Prescott & Crown King)

Shelley Ranch Cabin

Site of Stage Station

Wagoner Trail (To Crown King)

Minnehaha Creek

■ Lapham Place

Site of White Ranch

■ Graves (Lapham & Unknown)

Original Site of Lapham Place

Legend

Graded Road ——————

Primitive Road or Trail ‑ ‑ ‑ ‑ ‑

Drainage ‑·‑·‑·‑·‑

N

Fortuna Mine ■■

One Mile

(To Oro Belle)

Button Mine ■

(To Walnut Grove)

Boaz Mine ■

three carloads of mining equipment arrived in Prescott for the mine. In July, the mill frame at the Del Pasco was purchased from Diamond Jo Reynolds for the new operation, and a saw mill was set up at the Boaz to cut timber for the plant and buildings. Several of the owners of the Boaz Mining Company arrived in September from Fort Worth, Texas, to look over their mine and mill. By November, the new mill was completed and operating, and was said to be one of the finest ever put up in the Territory. Water for the mill was piped from Minnehaha Flat, three and a half miles away. In January, 1889, the Boaz Company was dissolved and reorganized, under substantially the same ownership as the Southern Belle Mining Company, but also included the mine of the same name that had belonged to Frank Ryland. Ryland had sold the Southern Belle mine to J. C. Rankin for $12,000 in October of 1888.

The new mill at the Boaz ran for several months without interruption, and regular shipments of bullion were leaving the mine. A Mr. David Boaz had been instrumental in securing the financing for the Boaz, or Southern Belle Mine, and he had also organized several other mining companies that were operating at Lynx Creek, Groom Creek, and on the Hassayampa. He had also sold a group of mines in Crook Canyon to investors from Dallas. In September, 1889, the Southern Belle Company became known as the Ryland Mining Company, and was in the process of adding twenty stamps to the already operating twenty stamps at the mill. By December, the company had thirty or forty men working at their mine and mill. This level of activity continued for the next year or so, but problems had apparently developed because the company was again reorganized in December of 1891. Claims against the company were paid off, and title to the property was transferred to H. L. Dufour. The name was changed to the Union Gold Mining Company.

In June, 1894, the Boaz mine and mill were leased to J. G. Ritchie, who operated the mill on ore from the Boaz and other nearby mines. S. C. Mott pumped out the main shaft of the mine, and found a respectable body of ore. Between the Boaz, A. T. Marsh's Fortuna mine and mill, and other mines, there were 100 men employed in the Minnehaha area.

The Fortuna Mining Company erected a ten-stamp mill in late 1892 and operated for a couple of years. In 1897, partners from a nearby mine repaired the mill and added concentrators, and later that same year the Fortuna itself was being operated by J. D. Moore under the ownership of Al McCann.

The Button Mine was also first mentioned in this time period. In May, 1898, William Button was working ten to twelve men on his property near Minnehaha, and by late 1899, he had constructed a steam hoist and was importing machinery for a mill.

In March, 1896, the legendary Sheriff Ruffner was summoned from Prescott to investigate a violent crime at Minnehaha. The Minnehaha storekeeper at the time was named Smith. On an evening in March, Smith and a neighbor, Lapham, were talking in the store. Two masked men burst in on them, and while one held Lapham from behind, the other chased Smith out the front door with gunshots. The one chasing Smith returned and the two intruders emptied the cash drawer. They then turned their attention to Lapham, beating him into unconsciousness with their gun butts. When Lapham came to, he grabbed his rifle, rounded up another local, and went looking for Smith. They found him near his own barn, shot to death. Tracks indicated that the two masked men had headed for Crown King, and it was suspected that a third man was involved. They had not touched Smith's safe, so murder, rather than robbery, was the suspected motive.

Besides the store and various mines in the area, there was also a successful cattle ranch at Minnehaha. It was established in 1883, when Fergus White moved his family onto a 160-acre homestead, and survived by selling meat to various Bradshaw mines, such as the Crown King. White died in 1895, but his wife and children remained to run the ranch themselves. His son, Jim, went to work in the mines, but was killed by bandits in 1905. Responsibility for the ranch fell to White's daughter, Kate, who became a famous roper. She later married a man named Bill Jackson, who helped run the ranch. The White ranch was located just across the drainage, to the west of where the Lapham house now stands. The only two buildings now standing in Minnehaha Flat are the Lapham cabin at the south end, and the Shelley Ranch line cabin at the north end. Lapham's house used to be about 200 feet south of its present location, in front of the graves. One of the graves is Lapham's, the other is of an unknown man who arrived in the area and died of an illness before anyone could find out who he was.

Chapter Thirteen:
The Silver Mountains and Humbug Creek

The Humbug Mining District was named for the reddish metal that was mistaken for gold by early placer miners on the Agua Fria. The metal proved to be bismuth, a mineral said to melt in boiling water.

For several years the rugged terrain and hostile Indians kept all but the hardiest miners out of this area, located on the southwest edge of the Bradshaws just a couple miles from the Tiger Mine. By the spring of 1874, there were twenty men mining and working arrastras on Humbug Creek. Fine, Martin and Moore had erected four arrastras on the creek, and had found ore worth $300 per ton. However, later that summer an incident occurred that confirmed the area's dangerous reputation.

In September of 1874, a man named William Roberts was murdered by three Indians along Humbug Creek. The Indians had been seen throwing tools down a mine shaft. As they were leaving the mine they happened upon Roberts at the creek. They shot him four times and stole his knife, guns, boots, and hat. The four other miners in the party heard the shots and ran up the creek, but the Indians had already fled. At first, it was suspected that the other miners had killed Roberts for his money. That rumor was laid to rest when Al Seiber, the famous scout, arrived at the camp with some of his Tonto Indian scouts. They examined the scene and decided that the Indians had been Apache Mohaves, and that there had been more than four of them. Seiber and his scouts, followed by troops from Camp Verde, tracked the Apache Mohaves and found them at the head of Cave Creek, north of Phoenix. Sieber's scouts came upon the Indians so suddenly that they had no time to call up the soldiers, so they fought the Indians themselves. Seiber and his men killed fourteen Indians, while suffering only one dead and two wounded.

Miners considered the Silver Mountains to be a prime area for prospecting since all of the gold and silver veins in the Bradshaws headed in their direction. A huge ledge, called the Mammoth, was indeed discovered there and was said to be 150 feet wide. However, the ore was of such a low grade that no large mine was ever developed in the Silver Mountains, in spite of the efforts of many miners over the years. The closest successful mines were the Tiger and Oro Bella at the south end of the Bradshaws across Humbug Creek, and the Boaz Mine to the west, toward Minnehaha Flat.

In 1883, the Mammoth Gold and Silver Mining Company was established to develop six claims of 1,500 feet each. The company's stock consisted of 200,000 shares at $5 each. The first 100,000 shares were to be sold as a development fund before any assessments were made. The 10,000 shares were sold in lots of not less than 100 shares at $1 each. It was hoped that with plenty of financial backing this huge vein could be turned into a profitable mine. It was indeed worked extensively at this time, but apparently nothing much came of it because within a year the area had again been forgotten about. In 1894, both the Mammoth and the Gray Eagle mines were sold to R. J. Turner for $500, indicating that neither had lived up to their original promise.

At one time there was a large and well-preserved example of a Chilean arrastra on the eastern slopes of the Silver Mountains. This was a more refined arrastra which involved the use of a large stone wheel to crush the ore rather than a rough-cut stone. The large wheel was removed from the site, and is now on display at the mining museum in Jerome. The canyon from which the mill was removed was subsequently named Wheels Canyon.

Chapter Fourteen:
The Tuscumbia Mine and Mill

Ed Gobin and James Mee purchased the Tuscumbia Mine, near Battle Flat, from a Mr. Lane around the new year of 1878. James Mee had set up the mill at the Peck, and then had gone to work at the Masterson mill on Turkey Creek. Ed Gobin was a storekeeper in Alexandra, and, in later years, had a saloon in Crown King. He had also been a foreman at the Peck. Lane is presumably the same man who developed the Lane Mine, and after whom Lane Mountain is named.

At first, ore from the Tuscumbia Mine was worked at the Masterson mill, and C. C. Bean's Aztlan mill near Prescott. In the spring of 1879, Mee announced his plans to construct a mill at the Tuscumbia. However, it was not until two years later, in March, 1881, that machinery for the mill finally started arriving at the millsite. The mill was to be constructed at Gus Swain's spring, about a mile and a half from the mine. It was a four-stamp mill with the capacity to expand to eight if required. Gobin ran the mine while Mee operated the mill. The mill was started up in June, 1881, and was said to work like a charm. It was estimated that there was $50,000 worth of silver ore in sight at the mine. After only a month of operation, the mill had shipped $30,000 worth of ore. The mill was also working ore from the Black Warrior Mine. In

early 1882, the town of Meesville, near the mill, was awarded a post office with James Mee as postmaster. There were forty men employed at the mine and mill.

In mid-1882, the Tuscumbia Mine and mill abruptly ceased operations in spite of its reported success. A year later, the mine and mill were purchased by the owners of the Black Warrior through their agent T. J. Eaman. Ore was packed into the mill from the Black Warrior and the Lane, which the Warrior company also owned. In 1885, Eaman, who had been running the mill, purchased the Black Warrior and Lane mines as well as the Tuscumbia mill, and continued to work all three. He also did custom work for other mines in the area.

In 1886 it was reported that Italian lessees of the Tuscumbia Mine had made a rich strike at the mine. Eaman, in the meantime, had moved to Camp Verde and branched out into the cattle business, and was said to have one of the largest stock ranges in Arizona. He held on to the Tuscumbia mill, however, and with Ed Gobin as operator, the mill was working ore from mines such as the Del Pasco as late as 1888. The foundation of the old mill can still be found beside Tuscumbia Creek, south of Battle Flat.

The Tuscumbia Mill on Tuscumbia Creek, near Battle Flat. Courtesy Sharlot Hall Museum

Chapter Fifteen:
Lane Mountain

The Lane Mine was located in approximately 1879 by James Lane on the southern slopes of what was later to become known as Lane Mountain. It was eventually to become closely tied to the operation of the Tuscumbia Mine, and its owner, T. J. Eaman, as mentioned in the previous chapter. Lane's original claim in the area was called the Three Sisters Mine, and he had driven a tunnel three hundred feet deep on it. Lane apparently had some mental problems, and was arrested by Sheriff Walker in 1881 on the charge of insanity. Although he continued his mining activities after this time, he was finally adjudged insane in 1885. Lane sold the mine to T. J. Eaman, the superintendent of the Black Warrior, for $20,000. It was mainly a silver mine, with ore said to be worth $200 to the ton.

Eaman began operations at the Lane in April, 1884, and in May, he had men working on a pack trail from the Lane to the Tuscumbia, so ore could be packed from the mine to the mill. He had 14 or 15 men working the Lane, and the ubiquitous Ed Gobin soon started a saloon at the mine. By June there were 100 animals packing ore from the Lane to the Tuscumbia mill. Within two months, 300 tons of Lane ore were crushed, with a dollar value of $50,000 to $60,000. However, the early promise of the Lane apparently was not a true indication, because by 1885, the year that James Lane was adjudged insane, all mention of the mine had ceased. The last news of James Lane was that he was working at the Tuscarora mine in the Tip Top area in 1886. There never was a road constructed to the Lane, but the current Lane Mountain Trail passes right by the old tunnel.

Another prominent feature on Lane Mountain is the Fat Jack Mine and cabin, nestled in the thick timber on the steep northwestern slope of Lane Mountain. It is said to have been located by a very thin miner nicknamed "Fat Jack" Campbell, who prospected the Bradshaws for many years with his portly partner "Slim Jim" Heath. The cabin on the claim is quite old and made of logs, and probably will not be standing for many more years.

Old log cabin on the Fat Jack Claim, Lane Mountain.

Chapter Sixteen:
The Oro Bella in the Early Days

The original mine in the area that is now known as Oro Belle, was the Oro Bonito, at the head of the canyon formed by Humbug Creek in the steep southwest slopes of the Bradshaws. It was developed by a group of California owners, and one of their first improvements was to bring in a ten-stamp mill. They authorized a contract to construct a road from Bradshaw City to their mine, in anticipation of the mill that was to arrive from California. The Bradshaw road builder, Jim Patterson, got the road contract, and in November, 1878, it was reported that the road had been completed, and that Patterson was hauling the mill from Walnut Grove. By January, 1879, the Oro Bonito mill had been started and was operating.

There is another version of this event that was told by Helen Harrington Sweet, the daughter of George Harrington who was later to own and operate the Oro Bella. Her recollection was that "Billy" Patterson was hired by Isaac Stoddard just to bring the mill equipment in to the mine for $17,000, but that in order to accomplish the task he would have to build a road. Patterson, however, outsmarted Stoddard by hauling the equipment on wagons with his bull teams to the top of Mount Wasson, overlooking the Oro Bonito, and then lowering the wagons with block and tackle down the steep slope to the mine. He sacrificed the wagons in order to avoid the job of building a road through the rough terrain. One inconsistency in this story is that the machinery was brought to the mine in 1878, but Isaac Stoddard's company did not buy the property until 1887. However, local residents have reported seeing the skid marks of the wagons on the slopes of Wasson Peak, and believe the story to be true.

In spite of all the trouble involved in getting the mill into the mine, the mill turned out to be a dud, and was said to be only good for grinding coffee. The owners then abandoned the mill and went back to working the ore with arrastras until they could afford to buy a decent mill. At one point, they had eight arrastras at the site.

A couple instances of violence colored the early Oro Bonito days. In June, 1879, a man named B. R. Vogt shot another man in the head. They had been drinking bad whiskey, and had gotten into a fight. The man died, and Vogt was convicted of manslaughter and sentenced to one year in the territorial prison. Samuel Clum, the superintendent of the Oro Bonito, committed suicide on July 2 by shooting himself in the mouth with a Colt pistol. He was said to be in bad health and over-taxed with responsibility. He had gone up a ravine to a sleeping tent, found the pistol, and then shot himself.

In the early 1880s, the mine was operated by G. W. Campbell. He had about six men working the mine, and was crushing ore in two steam arrastras. He worked Oro Bonito ore, and also did custom work at ten dollars per ton. This small scale operation, using arrastras to reduce the ore, continued until 1885. During this period, the Rapid Transit Mine was also being developed by J. N. Rodenburg in the Oro Bella area.

In late 1887, Isaac T. Stoddard, acting for an eastern syndicate, purchased the Oro Bella and Oro Bonito gold mines. The Notice of Incorporation of the Oro Bella Mining Company, with capital stock of $600,000, appeared in the Prescott paper on November 18, 1887. William B. Long was the foreman of the new operation, and there were plans to hire miners and erect reduction works in the spring. During the winter, several hundred feet of old workings were cleared, a large force of men

*Isaac T. Stoddard operated the Oro Bella
from 1887 to 1890.*
Courtesy Arizona Historical Foundation

began taking out ore, and houses and a mill
were soon to be built. This was the beginning
of the golden years of the Oro Bella Mine and
its surroundings.

In September, 1888, the Oro Bella
Company purchased the Wonder mill on Turkey Creek, and planned to move it to their
mine. They also were reported to have started
building a road into the mine. This supports
Mrs. Sweet's story that a road had not been
built to haul in the first mill. Isaac Stoddard
also arrived from the east to oversee all of this
activity. He had visited Washington D. C. to
get mail service for the new camp. It was
called Bayard post office and was established
on May 25, 1888, with William B. Long as
postmaster.

The mill from Turkey Creek had to be
moved back to Prescott and then around to
Walnut Grove, traveling ninety miles to cover
forty. Apparently, there was still no decent
road from upper Turkey Creek to the Crowned

King and Oro Bella areas. Long had seventy-
five men working at the mine and building the
road. By late October, 1888, the company had
fifty men working on the road from the mine to
Minnehaha Flat at a cost of $10,000. The old
Oro Bonito workings had been cleaned out,
and full operations were to be resumed once
the mill arrived and was started up.

By mid-December, 1888, the road was
completed and the company sawmill was busy
cutting lumber for the mill and other buildings.
However, muddy roads complicated the
freighting of machinery and equipment into the
mine. More machinery was also expected from
Chicago.

The freighters finally made the attempt
to reach the Oro Bella in February, 1889. By
May, the mill was finally installed, and was
said to be the finest in the county. Stoddard
himself replaced William Long as the superintendent of the mine, also hiring a Mr. Whiting
to run the mill, and Dudley Helm as the as-
sayer. The mill had cost about $40,000, and
the new road from Minnehaha to Bayard had
cost $13,000. Another $50,000 was spent on
developing and improving the Oro Bella and
Oro Bonito mines. Chutes were constructed to
move ore to the mill, thus avoiding transportation expenses. The company also planned to
add ten stamps to the mill to do custom work
for adjacent mines, and add concentrators as
well as equipment to treat ore by the chlorina-
tion process.

However, by June, the Oro Bella mill
faced the problem that plagued all operations
in the Bradshaws. Lack of water forced the
mill to shut down. There were said to be
thousands of tons of ore waiting to be processed. Also at this time, William Tyack became the foreman of the mines. Isaac Stoddard
and his wife returned to the east.

Little work was done at the mine or
mill until October, 1889, when J. Dudley
Helm was appointed as superintendent. By
December, the mill was running night and day.
In early 1890, the company purchased the
nearby Gray Eagle Mine, and started to build a

tramway from it to the Oro Bella mill. However, by June of 1890, the mill once again had to shut down for lack of water. In July, Isaac Stoddard resigned as president of the company, and J. D. Haynes, the vice president and general manager, arrived from the east. In August, Stoddard sold his interest in the company, ". . . for something handsome up in the thousands."27 After this shake up in the company, the mine lay idle for some time until V. K. Spear, representing the eastern owners, arrived and decided to resume operations. A crew of about twelve men worked on the mine through the winter of 1891-92. However, there were apparently problems with reducing the ore, and an experiment with the cyanide method proved unsatisfactory.

Another long period of dormancy followed at the Oro Bella. R. S. Barnes bought the mine in May, 1895. Later that year, a group that was leasing the Rapid Transit Mine leased the Oro Bella mill to work their ore, but no significant mining occurred for the next few years.

The Oro Bella camp looking west. The mill is the far building stretching up and down the slope. Courtesy Crown King Saloon

Chapter Seventeen:
The Peck Winds Down

Alexandra, the mining camp at the Peck Mine.
Courtesy Sharlot Hall Museum

Separate lawsuits filed against the Peck company by Ed Peck and Catherine Alexander were settled in favor of the company, thus allowing the company to plan a resumption of operations at the mine by late 1880. Stockholders in the company were assessed $1 per share. This also aroused hope that the mine would reopen. In April, 1882, the principal stockholders, Hobart and Hayward of San Francisco, sent a Captain Eagan to the East to try to organize the Peck company. At the same time, Mrs. Alexander withdrew all suits against the company, giving it clear title to the property for the first time in years.

By the summer of 1882, Alexandra was again a lively town. Under the direction of Captain Eagan, water was being removed from the Peck, and the Occident, next to the Peck, was also being developed. By October, the water in the Peck had been lowered to the hundred-foot level, and a vein of ore worth up to $10,000 to the ton in silver was discovered in the Occident. The Peck's hoisting works were repaired, and by September of 1883 the mill was again running with forty-five miners working the mine and mill. A letter to the *Prescott Courier* from a resident of Alexandra described its status in March, 1884, "The 'burg', just now, presents quite a lively appearance to a stranger. The saloons are full of men and money seems plenty. Drinking, poker and billiard playing going on day and night, and it might be supposed the 'old Peck' was a booming camp again, when the fact is that nearly everything has been at a standstill for several days past. More than a week ago the water coming down War Eagle Gulch began seeping into the Peck Mine faster than the hoisting works could take it out, and finally drove the miners out, and for five days only two engineers and two bucket tenders have been at work in the mine. The men were paid off as usual on the 5th inst. and are now taking a rest."29 As a result of the flooding of the mine, the operation was scaled back, but the mill continued to operate successfully on tailings through 1886. Regular transportation between Prescott and Alexandra was provided by Shill and Austin of the Gray Eagle Stables in Prescott. Bars of silver were sent regularly from the mill to Prescott, and the merchants in Alexandra were prospering. In early 1886, W. C. Dawes leased the Peck and began

pumping out the water. A new tunnel was started in order to strike the ore far below the surface. They pumped 40,000 gallons of water per day out of the mine. In April, a rich strike was reported, and the mill once again began working ore from the mine. By summer, Dawes had most of the water pumped out of the Peck, and mining and milling continued at a rapid pace. Captain Eagan brought in a large pump from San Francisco that was said to do the work of twelve men. In the election of 1886, sixty people voted at Alexandra. However, in spite of all this success, by September, 1887, the Peck was again idle. In the election of 1888, only sixteen voted at Alexandra.

The Peck saw another flurry of activity in 1889, when Captain Eagan worked the Occident on the Peck vein, but flooding again caused mining and transportation to shut down in early 1890. In 1895 and 1896, Achille Falco, who was later to work the Gladiator Mine, pumped out and operated the Peck for a time, but its glory days were definitely over. All in all, the Peck produced about $1,200,000 worth of ore in fifteen years of colorful and controversial operation. Its discoverer, Ed Peck, died a poor prospector in Nogales. C. C. Bean was defeated in his bid for a second term in Congress in 1886.

Chapter Eighteen:
Bradshaw Basin in the 1880's & 90's

After the decline of Bradshaw City and the Tiger Mine, activity in the southern Bradshaws began to center in the lower part of Bradshaw basin, near the present site of Crown King. By 1880, Bradshaw City was essentially a ghost town. A few log buildings remained into the 1890s, most notably a large dance hall built of hewn, four-square logs, with a whipsawed lumber floor that had been planed by hand. Its roof collapsed under heavy snow in 1894, and in 1900, it, and the other remaining buildings were reduced to wood for the Tiger mill. New claims were located in the area of the future Crowned King Mine. C. A. Luke's mill, eventually to become the site of the Crowned King mill, was operated by several different people over the years, including C. C. Bean of the Peck Mine. One of the principal

mine operators in the basin in this period was Orrin F. Place, who, as a partner in the Moody & Place mining company, worked the Buckeye, which was to become part of the Crowned King mine group, and the Union, which currently supplies Crown King with much of its water.

Luke's mill, referred to as the Bradshaw Basin mill, was leased by Bond and Hayden in 1884. They worked ore from their own mine, and did custom mill work for other miners. During this same period, J. Maslonski was elected justice of the peace with fourteen people voting in the election. John and Frank Luke were also developing mines in the area at this time, in partnership with their uncle, C. A. Luke, who was then a merchant in the Phoenix area. The Luke Mine was located in a saddle

The Basin Mill in about 1880 when it was operated by Bowen & Knowles.
Courtesy Sharlot Hall Museum

about two miles south of the Crowned King, and consisted of the Lorena, Cougar and Eclipse claims. The Bayard post office was located at the Luke Mine with John Luke as postmaster. A steam hoist was located on the Lorena claim where the main shaft was 300 feet deep. A crew of 25 men was working the mine in 1889. The present road between Crown King and Horse Thief Basin crosses this saddle, now called "Luke's hoist," just before the observation point overlooking Oro Belle. A depression just to the south of the road marks the location of this shaft. In the mid-1970s the shaft began to cave in, and the Luke family, which still owned the claim at the time, had to have it filled back in since it was so close to the road. Charles A. Luke died at the age of 67 in 1899. He had no children of his own, but was close to his nephews, Frank and John Luke. Frank was the father of Frank Luke, the famous World War I balloon buster and Congressional Medal of Honor winner, for whom Luke Air Force Base is named.

In 1886, Lester Jackson and John Curtin leased the Basin mill and used it to work ore from their operations at the Del Pasco and War Eagle mines. However, the summer of 1886 was the driest summer in memory, and the mill was barely able to operate at all.

In 1899, the Prescott Forest Reserve, which included the southern Bradshaws, was established by executive proclamation. In 1902, Crown King was to become the home of the first Ranger District in Arizona.

In 1900, Frank Murphy purchased mining property on the old War Eagle lode, and put men to work on a new shaft. There had been speculation for years that the Prescott and Eastern Railway would be extended from Mayer into the Bradshaws, but with the president of the railroad having a financial interest in the area, the construction of the railroad seemed certain.

Chapter Nineteen:
The Crowned King Mine

The largest mine in the Bradshaws, and the one that gave its name to the local settlement, was the Crowned King Mine. Years later, the name was shortened to its current form, Crown King. The first claim located in the Crown King group was the Buckeye, by Rod McKinnon on July 1, 1875.

O. F. Place had been developing his claims in the area of the future Crowned King Mine for some years, using contracted miners. He and a man named Moody were working the Buckeye claim in 1882 with six men. Local legend maintains that the first claim in the Crowned King group was discovered by a Walnut Grove schoolteacher named John L. Taylor who traded it to Place for a saddle (or saddle horse, depending on the version). Place then gave Bradshaw City storekeeper Noah Shekels a half interest in the claim in payment for a debt at the store. In any case, the vein continued to show promise, and in June, 1887, Place was visited by an eastern capitalist, George P. Harrington. Harrington had originally come to Arizona to investigate placer claims on Lynx Creek for a brother of Governor N. Oakes Murphy and railroad tycoon Frank Murphy. He came back to Arizona that fall, and in November returned to his home in Edinburg, Illinois, after spending a month in the Bradshaws with Place. He was said to have developed a very high opinion of the mines in the Bradshaws. Harrington, Place, and Shekels went on to form the Crowned King Mining Company on the basis of the work that Place and Shekels had done on their claims. They began filing applications for patents on mining claims in the area of the Crowned King in late 1887. Articles of Incorporation for the Crowned King Mining Company were filed in January, 1888.

Shekels, as superintendent of the new

George P. Harrington bankrolled the Crowned King Mine, and later operated the Oro Bella and Philadelphia Mines.
Courtesy Crown King Saloon

mine, erected a saw mill on the site in May, 1888, and began to assemble machinery for a ten-stamp mill, which was to start operation in July. The new mill was an expansion of Luke's original Basin Mill. A post office was established at the Crowned King in June, 1888, with George P. Harrington as the first postmaster. The mill actually began operation in August, and was said to be a very complete one. Shekels had fifty mules hauling ore from the mine to the mill, but as usual in the Bradshaws, operation of the mill was sporadic due to a scarcity of water. However, by late October, rains supplied plenty of water, and the mill was running day and night. The company also erected a store at the mine site at this time. Good ore continued to show up in the mine through 1889, and by the end of that year the company was piping in water for the mill, and was also building a road to connect the mine and mill. The present Crown King road passes right next to the remains of the mill's rock foundation about a half mile before reaching the Crown King store.

The early town of Crown King began to spring up along the road connecting the mine to the mill. Not surprisingly, one of the first business ventures was a saloon, operated by Ike Patrick, the same man who had been running the hoist at the Tiger in 1879 when the bucket dropped, killing and injuring several miners. Place applied for an injunction to restrain Sheriff "Bucky" O'Neill from issuing Patrick a license, because the establishment was proving to be too great a temptation for the men packing ore from the mine to the mill. A temporary injunction was issued, and the case was considered important because, if the injunction were sustained, it would allow prohibition without legislation. Obviously, Place

was not successful, since the road from the mine to the mill became the site for many such drinking establishments.

In February, 1890, the tremendous storm that washed away the Walnut Grove dam, causing one of the greatest disasters in Arizona history, also had an effect in Crown King. High water washed away $20,000 to $30,000 worth of concentrates, and damaged the mill enough that the boilers had to be reset.

The Crowned King mill continued to pound away at ore from the mine through 1890, at one point making three tons of highgrade concentrates per day. A wagon road was completed between the mine and Minnehaha Flat by way of the Tiger Mine, but bad roads continued to plague the mining operations in the southern Bradshaws. The Prescott *Weekly Journal-Miner* of January 7, 1891, called for a railroad to be built into the mountains to allow the mines to operate for the entire year.

The Bradshaw Basin Mill after being expanded to meet the needs of the Crowned King Mine. The surrounding forests were decimated to feed the boilers that drove the mill.
Courtesy Sharlot Hall Museum

Group at the Crowned King mill. In the back row, far left, is Noah Shekels, Crowned King Mine superintendent; third from the left is a bearded George Harrington; and on the right in the front row is Jack Nelson, Harrington's son-in-law and sometime deputy sheriff.
Courtesy Frances Pickett

After the usual scarcity of water closed the mill down for the first few months of 1892, the mine and mill reopened with a vengeance in April of that year when a 300-foot deep shaft was begun, a new assay office and other buildings were built, and the cyanide process was inaugurated in the mill. In the cyanide process, the ore was crushed to the size of a pea, and then put into a tank of cyanide solution where it was left standing for twelve hours. The solution was then pumped into a high tank and then leached through a box of zinc shavings which cleaned the metal from the solution. The solution lasted a long time, and could be used over and over. It was particularly useful in areas where water was scarce.

Unfortunately, as in the case of the Peck Mine, disagreements developed between the original developers of the mine. This time between George Harrington and Noah Shekels on one side, and Orrin F. Place on the other. Place had been the actual working superintendent of the mine and mill, while Harrington continued his banking business in Illinois. Harrington and Shekels believed that Place was not running the operation properly, and took over management of the mine. Place then

began litigation to regain control. When it was announced that the Crowned King Mining Company would hold its stockholders' meeting in Edenburg, Illinois, Place made an announcement in the Prescott paper that the meeting, at which Reuben Wilkinson, R. H. Hetherington, and George Harrington were elected directors, was not legal, and that acts and elections at the meeting were not valid. The notice was signed, "Orrin F. Place, President and Manager, Crowned King Mining Company." In January, 1893, the Crowned King was closed down by litigation. It was not opened again until October, 1893, and then with just a small force of men. Finally, in January of 1894, the mine was again operating with a full crew. The panic of 1893 caused George Harrington to close down his Illinois bank, and move his family to Crown King in 1894. He eventually paid off all depositors from his mine earnings.

The bad blood between Harrington and Place finally erupted into violence during the company's stockholders' meeting in Taylorsville, Illinois. Place became abusive toward Harrington and his attorney, James Taylor. Place tried to pick up his valise, which contained a revolver, but was restrained by

57

Taylor. Place struck Taylor on the head with his cane, and then pulled out the revolver and attempted to shoot Harrington. Bystanders struggled with Place and managed to prevent him from using the revolver.

Meanwhile, the mine operated successfully through 1894, and a half-million-dollar body of ore was discovered on the lower tunnel. The new town below the mine continued to grow, and Ed Gobin, formerly of Alexandra and the Lane and Tuscumbia mines, built a store at the town site. By early 1895, there were fifty men working at the mine. Another large body of ore was discovered on October, 1895, and by that time the mill had run constantly for almost a year, working thirty tons of ore per day. A constant supply of water was piped to the mill from the mine. The mine was turning out $40,000 to $50,000 worth of ore per month, and there were plans to add a new boiler and electric dynamo to supply light to the mine and mill. By July of 1896, the mine's light plant was in operation.

In mid-1896, the mine reduced its working force while sinking a deeper shaft, and establishing a station at the 400-foot level. They also built a boarding house, and improved the road from the mine to the mill. By November, the shaft was completed to the 500-foot level, and the mill was started up for the winter's run.

By this time, the area was populous enough to have its own deputy sheriff, and in January, 1897, Jack Nelson was reappointed as the resident deputy under Sheriff George Ruffner. Nelson was married to Essie Harrington, one of George Harrington's daughters. Many of Jack Nelson's descendents still live in Crown King. More of the history of the Harrington and Nelson families will be covered in a later chapter.

During the fall rainy season of 1897, an incident occurred that was to create one of the many lost treasure stories that endure in Arizona history. George Harrington, on the first leg of a visit to the east, was being driven in a buckboard to Prescott by experienced freighter J. P. Bruce. The buckboard also contained $5,000 in bullion from the Crowned King Mine. They had crossed the rain-swollen Wolf Creek, about six miles from Mayer, and were climbing the far bank when one of the horses balked. The buckboard slipped back into the water and overturned. Harrington managed to save himself by grabbing a tree branch, but Bruce and the horses were caught in the flood. Unable to find Bruce, Harrington walked to Mayer, and phoned to Prescott for help. A search party was sent out and Bruce's body was found about a half mile below the crossing at 1 a.m. the next morning. The bullion was never found, even though it was searched for extensively after Place accused Harrington of killing Bruce and stealing the gold.

By late 1897, the Crowned King Mine had a post office, a company store, several saloons, two Chinese restaurants, and a feed yard. The town lined the stage road that ran from the mine to the mill. The light plant at the mine kept the mill, mine, and town lit all night. In 1898, the Prescott & Eastern Railroad ran as far as Mayer, making transportation to the mines in the southern Bradshaws that much easier. In early 1899, a strike was made at the 500 foot level at the mine which was said to be one of the richest in Arizona history. The ore was valued at $180,000 per ton. It was so valuable that it was sacked in the mine, and put directly in the company's safe with extra guards to protect it.

In spite of the Crowned King's apparent success, the legal feud between the Place and the Harrington-Shekels factions of the company had more or less continued over the years, and finally resulted in the mine being shut down in 1899. Place had originally sued Harrington and Shekels for mismanagement after they had removed him as manager. He also charged them with fraudulent issuance of stock, and holding an illegal election and meeting of the board. Harrington and Shekels argued that this could not be settled in a local court since the company was an Illinois corporation. Judge Sloan of the Fourth Judicial

District accepted jurisdiction anyway, resulting in Harrington and Shekels suing Place and the Judicial District. Place eventually stopped trying to regain management of the mine after suffering a paralytic stroke. As in the case of the Peck, legal wrangling had resulted in the termination of a prosperous mining operation.

It has also been said, and later history seemed to bear this out, that the mine really closed down because the ore had played out. In spite of later attempts to reopen the mine, it never again became a large operation, and most later operations involved reworking the tailings when new technology made it profitable. In 1901, eastern investors bought the mine, and under the direction of George Shurtleff, installed a new electrical process at the mill in order to extract values from the tailings dump. This was apparently a failure.

In 1909, the mine was purchased by Frank Murphy at a receiver's sale for $35,000 in cash and $35,000 in stock. However, Murphy never actually operated the mine, being too involved in other areas of his railroad and mining empire. In 1916, Randolph and Gemmill, under the name of the Bradshaw Reduction Company, leased the mine, built a more modern mill, and reworked the tailings to produce a zinc concentrate. The mine was again operated from 1946 through 1948 by the Golden Crown Mining Company, which removed about 16,000 tons of new ore. As recently as the mid-1980s, the mine was again being worked, this time using a cyanide process to reduce the ore. Total production of the mine over the years was approximately $2,000,000.

With the closing of the original Crowned King operation, George P. Harrington, with his son Rube, turned his attention to the Oro Bella operation on Humbug Creek.

In this view looking south, the Crowned King mill is on the left . On the far right are the mine's assay office and company store. Poland Creek is in the center -- eventually the railroad followed its course. Courtesy Bob and Pat Schmidt

Chapter Twenty:
The Oro Bella and Humbug Country

The mill at the Oro Bella mine. Courtesy Crown King Saloon

George Harrington and his son, James R. "Rube" Harrington, took an option on the Oro Bella and Gray Eagle mines in 1900. Rube was shipping $250-to-the-ton gold ore, and was packing second-class ore to the Tiger mill to have it concentrated while the Oro Bella mill was being repaired. George Harrington moved his family to the Oro Bella in late 1900, and stayed there until June, 1901. The earlier history of the Oro Bella, or Oro Bonito Mine, was related in Chapter Sixteen. The Gray Eagle, near the Oro Bella, was located in 1871 by Jackson McCracken, one of the original locators of the Del Pasco. He sold the Gray Eagle to Phillip Richardson in 1872. Richardson continued to work the mine until the mid-1880s and was a prominent citizen of the Bradshaws for many years, but he went to work for the railroad in Prescott in 1886. He committed suicide in 1908 by shooting himself in the head twice with a .45 caliber cap and ball pistol. Apparently he was determined to die. He had been despondent ever since he had suffered a head wound the year before when the stove blew up in the sheriff's office.

After a satisfactory testing of the Gray Eagle and Oro Bella ore, an Illinois associate of Harrington's, Tom Lee, convinced the Illinois Retail Grocers Association to buy shares in the operation. The company was organized as the Tiger Gold Company with George Harrington as manager. A post office was established at the Oro Bella in 1904, and was called Harrington. Also in 1904, the construction of Frank Murphy's Bradshaw Mountain Railroad was approaching Crown King, so Harrington decided that a wagon road was necessary between the Oro Bella and Crown King. He hired Roscoe Willson, former historical columnist for *The Arizona Republic*, to boss the road construction crew. It was finished just before the railroad arrived. The present road to Oro Belle, which is what the ghost town at the mine is currently called, is still the steep route over Tiger Summit, built by Willson and his crew. The Tiger Gold Company also built a warehouse at the end of the rail line, in what was to become downtown Crown King. It was located approximately where the Crown King Realty building now stands. Next to the warehouse stood two large storage tanks that were only removed in the 1980s. Oil was brought up on the railroad and stored in the tanks for use by the railroad. It was also pumped over the ridge to the Oro Bella Mine to power the mill. While in operation, the pipeline was walked daily by Alfred Champie of the well-known Bradshaw ranching family, to check for leaks.

Harrington was an immensely popular manager of the Oro Bella, and could often be seen in overalls doing menial jobs around the camp. However, he was considered a bit of a spendthrift by the grocers in Illinois. As a result, in 1905, he was replaced by an engineer named Schlesinger who began a series of unpopular economical moves, such as reducing the quality and quantity of food at the boarding house. This continued until the whole crew finally confronted Schlesinger, threatening to quit if conditions didn't improve. Schlesinger, seeing the ruin of his career, broke down and agreed to meet all demands. Before long, Harrington was reinstated and the camp returned to normal. Harrington finally resigned in 1908, fed up with interference from stockholders. Harrington was a county supervisor at the time, and moved to Prescott. However, he

Roscoe Willson, right, on the porch of the Tiger Gold Company's warehouse at the end of the railroad in Crown King. Courtesy Crown King Saloon

eventually returned to Crown King and worked on other mines in the area until his death.

"Burro" John Revello, another, less reputable Bradshaw character, ran a whorehouse and saloon below Oro Belle, near where Humbug Creek crosses the present road. At that time the road was in the creek bottom and his saloon was about where the road now is. It was a popular place for women, cards, and drinks. Burro John was apparently quite a gunman, and was said to be able to shoot a deer at a distance with a pistol, and then would blow the smoke from the gun barrel in mock bravado. The clearing at the Prescott National Forest's southern boundary on Humbug Creek is referred to as Burro John, and is where he later lived with his wife. She had once been a prostitute in the "houses" of Crown King and the Oro Bella. There was a fairly substantial cabin in the clearing, but it was removed by the Forest Service in the mid-1970s.

There were a large number of buildings at the Oro Bella in the old days, including saloons, houses, a school, and the mill, along with various water tanks and utility buildings. A two-story boarding house stood next to the road until the mid-1970s when it finally succumbed to vandalism, as has the rest of the town. One rock wall of the boarding house still remains. Next to the boarding house there was a concrete building with a built-in safe. The safe still remains, but the door was stolen several years ago. The old, two-story saloon that now dominates downtown Crown King was dismantled and moved by burro from the Oro Belle in about 1916 by Frank Morgan, working for Tom Anderson. It had originally been located about a quarter mile up the canyon from the site of the boarding house, and its second floor had a rear door that was at ground level, as it had been built on the steep side of the canyon. The second floor rear door can still be seen at the back of the main part of the Crown King Saloon, although it now opens on thin air. As in most frontier saloons, the second floor was where the "girls" were headquartered. There was also a sawmill at the Oro

Belle at one time. The timber was cut in the vicinity of the Big Bell claim at the top of the canyon above the Oro Bella, and then skidded down the steep hill to the mill.

Don Van Tilborg, of an old Bradshaw family, had leased the Oro Bella for a time in the 1950s. He said that at that time, most of the original buildings at the mine were still intact, and most still had their window glass. He believes that the arrival of a jeep tour from one of the dude ranches in Wickenburg signalled the beginning of the end for the Oro Bella. There is virtually nothing left standing there today other than the one rock wall of the boarding house and the concrete walls of the old safe.

The road that follows Humbug Creek between the Bradshaw and Silver Mountains from the Oro Bella south to the Prescott National Forest boundary at Burro John passes some areas of historical interest, and some beautiful country. The road passes next to a large rusted boiler at the site of the long-abandoned Gazelle Mine. It skirts the jagged outcropping called Castle Rock, and then passes near the rock house where Charlie and

Al Francis, Bradshaw freighter and builder of "Fort Misery" on Humbug Creek. Courtesy Frances Pickett

Louise Kuder lived in the 1970s, while working their claim a hundred yards farther down the creek.

Where Jones Gulch opens onto Humbug Creek, there is an old cabin that was built by freighter Al Francis around the turn of the century. Francis hauled ore from the Oro Bella to the railroad in Crown King, and jokingly referred to his home as Fort Misery. It is still called Fort Misery, although Francis is long dead. An old cabin site, about a quarter of a mile south of Fort Misery, is known as Kentuck's place. Kentuck was a Civil War veteran named William Bell who lived there until he died in his 90s. The cabin had two stories, and was built into the side of the hill on the west side of the creek. When he died, he was buried on a hill across the creek. A tombstone was shipped to Crown King, and hauled to the Humbug by Al Francis. He and Burro John put the headstone on Kentuck's grave. The stone read, "Corpl. Wm. Bell, Co. E, 35th Kentucky Mtd. Inf." The last occupants of the cabin, while it was still habitable, were George Bigler

William Bell "Kentuck"
Courtesy Frances Pickett

and his wife, who were there into the late 1960s.

Al Francis' "Fort Misery" in the 1920s.
Courtesy Frances Pickett

Chapter Twenty-One:
The Railroad and Middelton

The arrival of Frank Murphy's Bradshaw Mountain Railway in Crown King in 1904 brought drastic changes to both the appearance and location of the town. The town had originally been built along the road between the Crowned King Mine and the Crowned King mill, but the railroad and its buildings formed the nucleus of the new town, in the lowest and flattest part of Bradshaw Basin. The Bradshaw Mountain Railway included the branch to Crown King, as well as a branch to Poland, at the northeastern edge of the Bradshaws. The main line was the Prescott & Eastern that ran from Prescott to Mayer. Frank Murphy had been the driving force behind getting a modern railroad built from Ash Fork to Prescott, the Congress Mine, and Phoenix. One of his earliest investors was "Diamond" Jo Reynolds, who, besides owning the Congress Mine, had been an investor in the Del Pasco Mine in the southern Bradshaws. The Prescott & Eastern was completed to Mayer in 1898, and its success encouraged Murphy to consider continuing the railroad into the mineral-rich Bradshaws. Miners and merchants had been clamoring for a railroad to be built into the Bradshaws for years. Primitive means of transportation had been a major drawback to the development of mines in the area since the first discoveries in the 1860s. However, the means and interest did not exist in such an ambitious venture until Murphy became involved in local mines such as the War Eagle lode, on which he bought property in 1900. As organizer and president of the Prescott National Bank, he had arranged loans for the Bashford-Burmister Mercantile Company, which had also had interests in Bradshaw mines for years.

The Poland branch was completed in

Railroad construction camp in Crazy Basin. Switchbacks will ascend the slope in the background. Courtesy Frances Pickett

The crew lays rail across the trestle at the gap just outside Crown King.
Courtesy Crown King Saloon

1902, and work on the Crown King branch was begun. Other than the section through Cedar Canyon, between Mayer and Cleator, construction was not particularly difficult until the crews reached Crazy Basin. At this point the country became rough and steep, and numerous switchbacks were necessary to ascend the mountainsides. A construction camp with a turntable was established at the northern end of Crazy Basin below the DeSoto Mine. The station was named Middelton after George Middleton, who owned the DeSoto. The spelling was changed by the railroad. A crew of up to 600 men was required to finish the line to Crown King. Work was further hampered by the severe winter of 1903-04, but the rails finally reached Crown King, and scheduled trains began arriving at the new depot in May, 1904.

The DeSoto was a copper mine, and with the arrival of the railroad in Crazy Basin in 1903, a new tunnel was established at the mine, and an assay office, boardinghouse, cookhouse, blacksmith shop, warehouse, and corral were built high on the slope overlooking Middelton. In order to expedite transportation

from the mine to the new railroad siding, the mine owners built an aerial tramway that was completed in April, 1904. It was designed by the Blechert Transportanlagen Company of Leipzig, Germany, was four thousand feet long and could carry two thousand tons or ore per day.

Middelton also became the main construction camp for the Bradshaw railroad, and besides temporary construction crew quarters, the railroad also built a permanent section workers' bunkhouse, and a house for the foreman and his family. They also constructed a depot, a station agent's house and two other dwellings, a water tank, tool shed, and other storage buildings. There was also a temporary turntable built for use during construction. Also in town were the tram terminal and powerhouse of the DeSoto, a Wells Fargo and Western Union office, and a post office established on May 8, 1903, with George Middleton as postmaster. In 1904, there were seventy-five people in Middelton and one hundred at the DeSoto.

Frank Murphy, the power behind the building of the railroad, knew Middleton, and

65

Bradshaw Mountain Railway trestle in Crazy Basin. The cut at the far end of the trestle is still easily visible from the Crown King Road. Courtesy Crown King Saloon

by 1905 was on the board of directors of the Arizona Smelting Company, which owned the DeSoto.

There were two saloons in Middelton, one owned by Thomas Hogan, and the other by Robert Schwanbeck. Neither establishment lasted long, and Schwanbeck eventually moved to Humboldt.

After the railroad stopped making scheduled runs to Crown King and before the rails were removed, residents used horse-pulled rail cars to travel and transport goods to and from Middelton. Courtesy Crown King Saloon

A Bradshaw Mountain Railroad train entering Crown King. The Crown King mill smokestacks are in the right rear. See the following page for another picture of the same area.
Courtesy Crown King Saloon

Before long, the company operating the DeSoto went bankrupt, and, in 1908, the post office was discontinued and many of the buildings were boarded up. Only a mine watchman and a few railroad employees were left in the once busy town. The ore in the mine had proven of insufficient quality to maintain a large operation. Two of the railroad buildings were leased to a rancher.

World War I greatly increased the demand for copper, and new technological advances and mining methods made it once again profitable to open the DeSoto. The tramway was reconditioned, and life returned to the town. However, it did not return to its former level of activity. The only business in town, besides the railroad, was a small store that James Cleator operated in part of a railroad warehouse. The mine office had moved to the DeSoto itself. The post office was re-established in 1916 and was called Ocotillo, with Pearl Orr of the local ranching family as postmaster. A schoolhouse was built in 1917

for all eight grades, but the maximum enrollment was fourteen pupils. Approximately two hundred people lived in the town during World War I.

Increased mining activity kept the town and railroad busy during the war, but in the early twenties many of the mines in the Bradshaws were abandoned, and work at the DeSoto was discontinued in 1922. It had produced $3,250,000 worth of copper ore. The Ocotillo post office was discontinued in 1925, and in 1926 the railroad tracks between Middelton and Crown King were removed. The railroad removed the tracks to Middelton in 1932 as well as all the structures that it had occupied. The only structures still surviving today are a few of the tramway towers.

During the last years of the railroad, when rail service between Middelton and Crown King was sporadic or nonexistent, residents of Crown King used a wagon with railroad wheels to transport themselves and their supplies between the two towns. They would use a horse to pull the wagon up the mountain, and coast on the way down, using a hand brake to control the wagon's speed. Elsie Van Tilborg, an early Crown King resident, remembered taking the train to Middelton after a hospital stay in Prescott. She stayed at the Orr ranch, which was in Middelton at the time, and then was taken to Crown King by her husband, Glen, on top of a load of hay in the wagon. "I got sunburned," she said.30

The present road between Cleator and Crown King closely follows the old railroad bed. However, here and there you can see the former rail line off to either side, particularly where the vehicle road drops into a drainage that had once been spanned by a trestle. Approximately two miles outside of Crown King, at a sharp curve of the road where an observation point overlooks "Hells Hole," the ridge was penetrated by a railroad tunnel, the collapsed ends of which can still be seen. The tunnel now contains the former contents of the Crown King dump, which once marred the scenery just outside of town on the steep slope of Poland Creek, next to the road. The dump was cleaned up at the behest of the Forest Service in the mid-1970s.

Essentially the same scene as in the previous photograph, but from a slightly different angle. The row of buildings on the left appear in photos dating back to the 1880s. The Crown King Mine assay office and store are on the right.
Courtesy Crown King Saloon

Chapter Twenty-Two:
The Towers Mountain Area

Towers Mountain is the highest point in the southern Bradshaws at 7,628 feet. It can be easily identified by its array of microwave and radio relay towers, as well as a Forest Service lookout tower. It is located about three miles northwest of Crown King, and is about one mile west of the Del Pasco Mine, one of the first big strikes in the Bradshaws. The name of the mountain apparently goes back farther than the towers that now festoon it. A miner named George Tower worked the Green Mountain Mine near the meadow on the west side of the mountain in the late 1880s to early 1890s, between trips to insane asylums, that is. The first mention of Tower was in 1883, when he was declared insane, and sent to Stockton, California. He was living in Walnut Grove at the time. In 1891 he was living in the Bradshaws, and was again adjudged insane and sent to the asylum in Phoenix. He believed that he was being pursued by enemies who wanted to kill him with electricity. He died in the asylum in 1894.

The meadow that Tower lived in has come to be known as the "spud ranch" over the years, since various owners have grown famous crops of potatoes there. One of the Prescott newspapers reported that, in August, 1894, Sandy Vaughn and J. E. Reynolds had a fine crop of potatoes at the Tower ranch. One of the ranch's owners around the turn of the century was "Blanco" White, who came to an untimely, if not somewhat comical, demise. He was growing potatoes for the local mines when the following events, as told by Helen Harrington Sweet, occurred. "Blanco White owned the Spud Ranch on Towers Mountain for a time and had it planted in potatoes. He went to Bully Bueno to deliver potatoes, and found himself in the middle of a party. One of the crowd was the possessor of a fiddle from

which he persistently drew doleful and lugubrious wails of which his companions grew very tired so when he laid his fiddle down and absented himself for a short time, Blanco seized the opportunity to give the fiddle bow a liberal application of soap. This did not appeal to the violinist at all and during the altercation that ensued he hurled a beer glass at the luckless Blanco, striking him in the forehead and fracturing the skull from which he died a few days later. His assailant was not convicted due to the fact that Blanco got out of bed after being hurt and sustained a fall, thereby creating a doubt in the minds of the jurors as to the real cause of the fracture."[31]

In 1916, George P. Harrington operated a saw mill on Towers Mountain to saw timber for the tramway he was building from the Wildflower Mine to the Crown King mill. The site of this sawmill can still be located on the northwest slopes of the mountain by the huge piles of decaying bark that still remain. The Wildflower Mine was located in a deep gulch on the north side of the saddle between Towers Mountain and Del Pasco Ridge. The Gemmill brothers, Mark and Dave, operated the Wildflower between about 1910 and 1916. There was no mill at the Wildflower, so they built, or had built by Harrington, an aerial tramway that ran from the mine to the mill at Crown King. The mill was operated solely on Wildflower ore at this time. After finishing their work on the Wildflower, they reworked the tailings at the Crown King mill. The Gemmill's later operated the big pit at Jerome on a small scale for about 15 years and got rich. Some signs of the Wildflower tram can still be found. From the mine, you can still barely make out the break in the trees in a straight line up Del Pasco Ridge to the southeast. On top of the ridge some of the collapsed towers can still be found with

The line of the Wildflower tramway can be plainly seen running from its terminus at the Crown King mill to the top of Del Pasco ridge. The first tower can be seen just above the roof of the tram station next to the mill. Courtesy Frances Pickett

rusted running gear lying around. The heavy metal cable that carried the aerial ore cars is still stretched on the ground over much of the tram's route.

Another important mine on Towers Mountain was the Buster Mine, located on the mountain's steep west slope, overlooking North Pine Creek and the old stage stop at Hooper. It was a copper mine that was originally located by T. W. Boggs and D. R. Poland, but nothing more than development work was done on it. In 1892, a Captain Burgess, with what was thought to be English money behind him, bought the mine and planned to hire a large crew to erect an expensive mill and work the mine. However, little apparently came of Captain Burgess' plans, because a mill was not erected at the mine until nine years later. In 1895, the mine was owned by J. A. Forbes and

John McKenzie, who sold the Buster and Standard mines to Baltimore investors for $33,500 in 1899. By the middle of 1899, a mill had been built at the Buster and was operational, and there were 65 men working on the property. Early 1900 saw the mill shut down for an extended period due to the problem that plagued all Bradshaw operations, lack of water. However, by May of 1900, the mill was working 30 tons of ore per day. In 1926, the Buster was owned by Charles Swazey. It then had three tunnels, the longest being 400 feet. The Buster Mine was apparently not a great success, since little more is mentioned of it. There are still traces of the mine, including a dilapidated shack or two, high on the western slopes of Towers Mountain.

After the death of Blanco White, the next known inhabitants of the Towers ranch

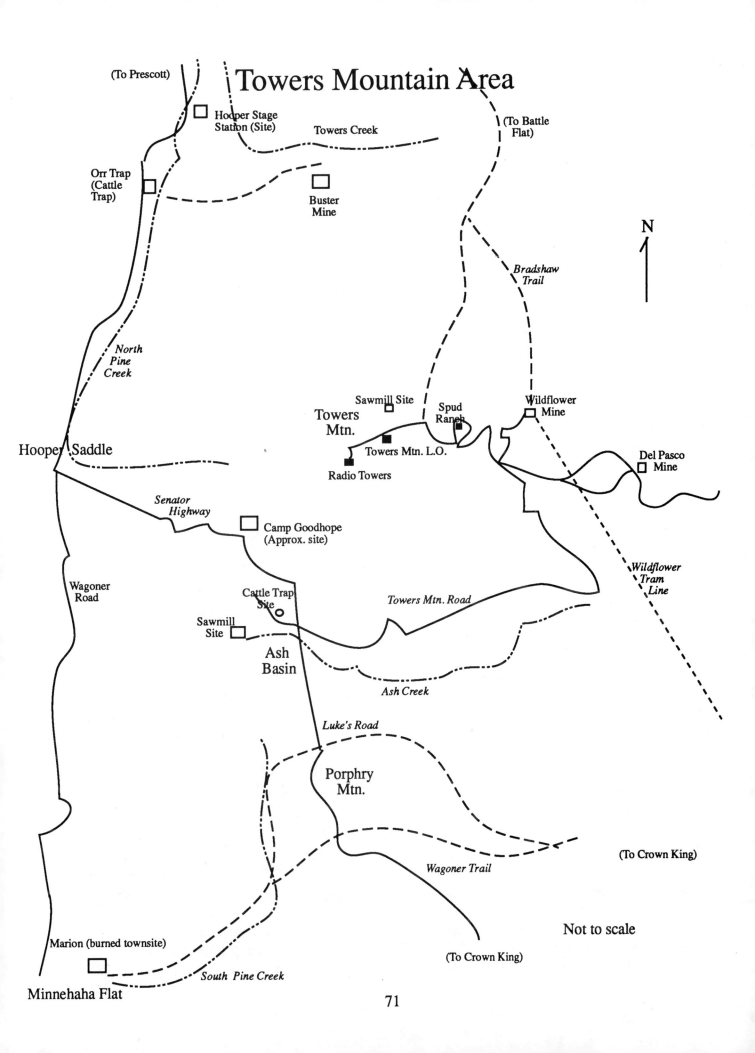

Towers Mountain Area

(To Prescott)

Hooper Stage Station (Site)

Towers Creek

(To Battle Flat)

Orr Trap (Cattle Trap)

Buster Mine

N

Bradshaw Trail

North Pine Creek

Sawmill Site

Spud Ranch

Wildflower Mine

Towers Mtn.

Del Pasco Mine

Hooper Saddle

Towers Mtn. L.O.

Radio Towers

Senator Highway

Camp Goodhope (Approx. site)

Wagoner Road

Wildflower Tram Line

Cattle Trap Site

Towers Mtn. Road

Sawmill Site

Ash Basin

Ash Creek

Luke's Road

Porphry Mtn.

(To Crown King)

Wagoner Trail

Not to scale

Marion (burned townsite)

(To Crown King)

Minnehaha Flat

South Pine Creek

were the family of Glen and Elsie Van Tilborg, who moved to the Crown King area from Nevada in 1919 to help a friend work a mine near Towers Mountain. The Van Tilborg's were originally from the Colorado Springs area, and Glen had worked as a miner at Cripple Creek as a youth. They had two sons, Grant and Don. Don was about four at the time, Grant was a baby, and a daughter, Mildred, was born in Prescott in 1921. They drove up from Prescott in a car on the Senator Highway. The Towers Mountain mine did not work out so the Van Tilborg's bought Tower's ranch and moved onto it. They bought the ranch in 1925 from a man named Funk, who had inherited the property and had never seen it. The previous year they had purchased a house and land in Crown King. While owning both properties for many years, they began a long practice of spending their winters in Crown King and their summers in the "high country" at the Towers ranch. There was a new cabin in the meadow that they moved into, and next to it was an old log cabin that had been there, they were told, since about 1864. The cabin was still in good shape at that time, with furniture inside, along with an ancient Confederate flag. The Van Tilborg's grew potatoes on the land while Glen worked at various mines in the area.

Their son Don rode a burro to school in Crown King every day from Towers Mountain. He left his burro in the stable under the Tiger Gold Company's warehouse in downtown Crown King. He went to the current schoolhouse, but the original schoolhouse was on a flat where the Philadelphia spur rail line crosses the road to the Crown King Mine, just below the site of old Crown King.

Don remembers that when he was young, there was a man who was known as Crazy Smith who had a settlement named Camp Goodhope on the south side of Towers Mountain. Smith went everywhere leading a string of burros with empty packs. Glen Van Tilborg had located a claim near Smith's claims, so Smith came to the spud ranch to complain. Glen was not there, so Smith took his anger out on Don, shouting and waving his rifle at him. Luckily, an old buffalo hunter and Indian fighter named Jim Lewis was staying with the Van Tilborg's at the time, and he came out to see what the commotion was. Seeing Smith, he pointed his finger at him and told him to stay right where he was. He then ran back to get his rifle. Smith, apparently knowing Lewis' reputation, beat a hasty retreat. Lewis spent the rest of the day patrolling the mountain top, but Smith did not return. Lewis lived with the Van Tilborg's periodically over the years, and died at their ranch in Crown King. He spent his last years as a woodcutter. Eventually, the Van Tilborg's main occupation was operating a cattle ranch that they had established, headquartered on their property in Crown King.

The log lookout tower on Towers Mountain, built around 1919.
Courtesy Crown King Saloon

Because of its height and strategic location, the Forest Service constructed a crude wooden lookout tower on the peak of Towers Mountain around 1919, followed in the 1930s by a more permanent tower that is still in use. Along with the tower, a one-room cabin, horse stable, and corral were built. The original lookout concept in the Forest Service was for a couple to live at the tower with the wife acting as the lookout, and the husband as a one-man fire crew. When the wife spotted a fire, the husband would jump on a horse and ride to the fire, fighting it strictly with hand tools for as long as was necessary. One of the preferred methods of constructing a fire line was to lasso a log and drag it behind the horse around the fire.

Orr Trap, a corral beside the Senator between Hooper Saddle and the old stage station of Hooper, was called Forsyth Flat in the early 1900s. At Hooper, there was a stage station, two or three houses and a stamp mill.

There was a saw mill on Ash Creek below Towers Mountain, but there are only the remains of a wrecked house there now. The flattened house can still be found about a

Don Van Tilborg

quarter mile down Ash Creek from where the Senator Highway crosses it on the southwest side of Towers Mountain.

The Spud Ranch was sold by the Van Tilborg's to the Collup family, who still own it. The old log cabin, which the Van Tilborg's first saw in 1919, is still there.

An aerial view of Towers Mountain in the 1970s Courtesy Prescott National Forest

73

Chapter Twenty-Three:
The Gladiator Mine

The Gladiator Mine was located on the north end of the War Eagle lode, which had lain dormant for several years. The Jackson brothers had worked in the area during the early Del Pasco days. In 1892, two men named Blauvelt and Watts obtained a bond on the Gladiator. They hired a crew to clean out the old workings and develop new crosscuts. They claimed to have $350,000 to $400,000 worth of ore blocked out, and were finding more daily. They were working their ore at the Del Pasco mill, and in July of 1892, they had fifty tons of their ore at the old Del Pasco.

In late 1893, the Gladiator was sold for $50,000 to investors from Colorado. Achille Falco, one of the owners, was named manager of the new operation, and a ten-stamp mill was ordered almost immediately. By February, 1894, the new company had thirty-six men working at the mine, and by May, the mill was up and operating, slowed down by the Bradshaw's usual lack of a reliable source of water. Falco's company continued to operate the Gladiator successfully through 1897, and also became involved in trying to pump out and reopen the Peck Mine. Falco was a "remittance" man from France. His wealthy parents, estranged from him due to his marriage, paid him to stay out of his homeland.

In 1897, in order to overcome the lack of water during the summer droughts, the company installed water tanks, pipe, and a

The Gladiator Mill, built in 1894. Courtesy Crown King Saloon

The remains of the Gladiator stamp mill in Crown King. The small house in the background was built by Jack Sweet for his new bride, Helen Harrington Sweet, George Harrington's daughter. It was known as "the house that Jack built."

pump to get water from the head of Peck Gulch. The mine's crew in the winter of 1905-06, included Roscoe Willson, and future long-time residents and saloon keepers in Crown King, O. A. "Doc" Tyler, and Tom Anderson.

The Gladiator has been reopened from time to time over the years, but most of the activity there occurred in the 1890s to just past the turn of the century. In 1939, E. M. Moore and Sons leased the mine and turned out about 4,500 tons of ore per year for the next decade. They had originally shipped their ore directly to smelters, but in 1945, they bought the Golden Belt mill on Turkey Creek, east of Cleator, and trucked their ore there to be worked.

The stamp mill that had been installed in 1894, was left at the mine and could still be

seen, in some semblance of its original state, until 1985. At that time, the Gladiator was taken over by the Norquest Company, which cleared out all of the remaining buildings and equipment and installed a modern mill and concentrator. The company worked the mine with a forty to fifty man crew for the next three years, making it the largest mining operation in the Bradshaws for many years. The remains of the old stamp mill were moved to Crown King, and some local residents hoped to rebuild it as an historical display. However, parts were missing, and a great deal of work would have been required to reconstruct it, so it was never done. The remains of the mill are now piled next to the road just past Harrington's former home and the old Crowned King Mine assay office.

Chapter Twenty-Four:
Bumble Bee

The first area in the southern Bradshaws to be explored and mined by the earliest Mexican and American intruders was around Bumble Bee. It was here that William Bradshaw came with a few followers to test the placering possibilities of Turkey and Black Canyon Creeks, and it was here that the first mining districts in the Bradshaws were established in 1864: the Bradshaw and Turkey Creek Districts. Transportation difficulties and hostile Indians prevented development of the area, as the miners moved upstream to concentrate on the lode claims in the mountains where the "float" in the low country had come from.

There are several legends about how Bumble Bee got its name. One legend is that some of the first miners in the area stumbled on a bee hive in cliffs near Black Canyon Creek and named the drainage Bumble Bee Creek. Another, is the same legend but substituting soldiers for miners. A third version states that some Army scouts were in the area and heard a gathering of Indians that was so large that the noise they made sounded like a hive of bees. In any case, the drainage that empties into Black Canyon became known as Bumble Bee Creek, and the stage station established on its banks by the spring was called Bumble Bee Station. The original station was an adobe building beside the creek, among the willows, about a quarter mile east of the bridge that spans the creek to the south of the town's current location. It served the traffic between Prescott and Gillette, at the Tip Top Mine to the south of the Bradshaws, and between Prescott and the tiny community of Phoenix. A post office was established in Bumble Bee and the first postmaster was William D. Powell, who was appointed on February 3, 1879. The best-known station keeper at the Bumble Bee station was Warner

W. Snyder, who became postmaster on June 15, 1880, and ran the stage station for many years. One of the early miners in the area was Henry Wickenburg, of Vulture Mine fame. After leaving the town that now bears his name, he came to the Bumble Bee area and developed the Iconoclast Mine, about four miles south of Bumble Bee, in 1881. It was located on Arrastra Creek, which is the drainage that the road connecting old Highway 69 and Interstate 17 follows.

In 1887, a rather lurid incident occurred near Bumble Bee that involved two Texas families passing through town in their wagons. The Brices and Whitneys, who had twelve children between them, were camped on a hill just south of Bumble Bee when Whitney decided that he wanted to swap wives with Brice. When Brice refused, Whitney pulled a gun on him and forced Brice into his own wagon with Mrs. Whitney. As Brice was climbing into the wagon, Whitney grabbed a shovel and struck him over the head with it, killing Brice. Whitney fled, and there was no subsequent story of his capture.

Activity apparently slowed down at Bumble Bee shortly after Snyder took over, and on February 1, 1888, the town's post office was discontinued. This action must have been unpopular, because the post office was reestablished in June of the same year, with Snyder reappointed as postmaster.

There was a resurgence of mining activity in the Bumble Bee area during the 1890s. A five-stamp mill was operating at the Blouchouna Mine, three miles south of Bumble Bee; the Ballard brothers were working the 88 Mine; Meyers, James, and Webb were working the Oro Fino; and McFee and Corruthers were working a claim one mile north of the town. There was talk of installing a hydraulic plant to wash gold out of the creek bottom. In 1900, George W. Middleton, who was later to operate the DeSoto Mine, was working three shifts on the Zika property. However, there were never any large mining operations in the Bumble Bee area, and the only real excitement came with the initial discoveries of placer gold along Black Canyon in the 1860s.

The next businessman to locate in the area was Jeff Martin, the storekeeper in Canon, now known as Black Canyon City, who put about a thousand head of cattle on some land he had purchased near Bumble Bee in about 1918. Martin was originally from Missouri, but came to Arizona as a miner via the gold fields at Cripple Creek, Colorado. While working at the Monarch Mine in the Cherry Creek area, he met and married Edna Marr, daughter of Dennis Marr, one of the pioneer cattlemen of the Verde Valley.

Jeff Martin, Bumble Bee storekeeper.
Courtesy Crown King Saloon

After Jeff Martin had established his cattle operation in Bumble Bee, he built himself a store there. He continued to operate his store at Canon, and spent a great deal of time commuting between the two businesses.

However, his expansion turned out to be too ambitious, and he overextended himself financially. In the early 1920s, the bank foreclosed on his mortgage, and Jeff was forced to choose which property he would keep and which he would turn over to the bank. Thinking that Bumble Bee had a brighter future, he turned his property at Canon over to the bank and retreated to Bumble Bee, where he was to spend the rest of his life. Subsequent growth of Black Canyon City, and the re-routing of the state highway onto Black Mesa, proved Martin's choice to be the wrong one.

Martin's original store was called "The Beehive," and was located about a quarter mile upstream from the original stage stop. The road had originally run along the east side of Bumble Bee Creek, and then up the ridge top heading south, past the spring where Snyder's had been located. However, there was a bad drainage crossing on this route and the road was moved, sometime in the twenties, to its present location, except that it still crossed the creek near Snyder's and continued along the ridge top. Martin then had to tear down his store and move it to a new location near the old stage stop. At this location, he added some small rental cabins.

Another violent incident occurred in the Bumble Bee area in 1929 that directly involved Roscoe Willson, who wrote about it in his historical column in the *Arizona* magazine. Willson was temporarily staying in Bumble Bee, sleeping in an outbuilding with Martin's two teenage sons, Joe and Vernon. At the same time, a herd of sheep was passing through Bumble Bee on the way from the desert to the summer grazing in the high country. Several of the herders had managed to get a hold of some moonshine, and had gotten involved in a drunken quarrel near Martin's store. Several of the Mexican herders were picking on a one-armed Yaqui herder named Jose Gutierrez, nicknamed "El Mocho." Martin, who heard the raised voices from his store, went to where they were arguing and suggested that they return to their camp.

Knives had already been pulled, and Martin feared that someone was going to get killed. The herders left, but sure enough, in the middle of the night someone returned to the store from the herders' camp and told Martin that Gutierrez had shot Juan Chacon. The talking roused Willson and the Martin boys, who got up to see what all the excitement was about. Martin sent the man from the camp to

passed when the "WPA's" built a new bridge across Bumble Bee Creek, and moved the road down from the ridge top to its present location, contouring the west side of the ridge as it headed for Canon. Martin moved again, this time building the store that still stands today. He had it constructed out of porous malpais rock that his son, Vernon, hauled from across the creek. This happened in about 1935. He

Cordes to call the sheriff in Prescott. At about noon the next day, a deputy sheriff and several of the herders, including the accused killer, arrived at the store with Chacon's body. An attorney named Patterson conducted an informal inquest, with Roscoe Willson as one of the "jury." What had happened was that, as Gutierrez was riding by the Chacon's campsite, he was stopped by Juan Chacon, who tried to get him off his horse to fight with knives. Gutierrez resisted, and in the struggle he pulled out his rifle and shot Chacon in the chest. When Chacon fell, Gutierrez fired four more shots into him. He then returned to his own camp. After this inquest, the killer was taken to Prescott. He was tried and convicted of first degree murder and sentenced to life in prison.

In the 1930s, Martin was again by-

also put the rental cabins on skids and hired the county road crew, which had a work camp at the south end of town at the time, to haul them to the new location. They were only one room cabins, but have subsequently been added on to.

By the 1940s, Jeff Martin's empire had shrunk to just forty acres around the store, which included the rental cabins and the Martins living quarters across the road. He had previously sold land to Fred and Claire Cordes when they moved their FF Ranch headquarters from near Cleator to Bumble Bee. The existing house, across the road from the store, was built in 1945 on the same foundation as the previous house, which had been destroyed by a fire that nearly killed Vernon Martin's family. The rock school house, now a home, was built

The Martin house in Bumble Bee. It was rebuilt by Vernon Martin in 1945 after being destroyed by a fire.

Vernon Martin

by the CC's during the thirties. By the 1940s, Jeff had become too old to run the store, and it was operated by a series of lessees. Jeff died in the late forties at the age of 76, and in 1948 his widow, Edna, sold Bumble Bee and moved to Prescott. Their son, Vernon, now lives in Crown King and has spent much of his life working as a miner and ranch hand in the southern Bradshaws.

The appearance of Bumble Bee was substantially changed when the new owner, Charles A. Penn, built a fake ghost town on the north side of the old store. People could walk through the "town," but only the store itself was actually in operation. In 1969, Phoenix restauranteur "Crazy" Ed Chilleen secured a long-term lease from Penn. He planned to promote Bumble Bee as a ghost town resort, and began by adding an open-air restaurant. There was a grand opening of the new tourist attraction in November, 1969, attended by 4,000 people, and sixty newsmen. There was a saloon, trading post, photo shop, blacksmith

shop, shooting gallery, assay office, and a stable and barn where antiques were sold. There was even a souvenir newspaper called the *Bumble Bee Buzz* , and a twenty-four room hotel was planned. Activities included gold panning, horseback riding, and dancing. In spite of all the hoopla, and all the money spent, the town never really caught on as a tourist attraction. Chilleen guessed that this was because the town's only historical significance was as a stage stop, and, of course, due to the the five miles of dirt road between the highway and the town.

For the past fifteen to twenty years there has been little activity in Bumble Bee, other than at the FF Ranch, now called the Bumble Bee Ranch. There have been sporadic attempts to reopen the store, but most tourists only seem to speed through town in their air-conditioned vehicles on the way to the cooler heights near Crown King and Horse Thief Basin.

The Bumble Bee store and some of the rental cabins as they look today.

Chapter Twenty-Five: Cleator

Cleator began its existence as a railroad work camp in 1902 when the Bradshaw Mountain Railway was being built. Seeing a business opportunity on the new railroad, Mayer lumber company owner Leverett Nellis bought land at what was then called Turkey Creek Station, and started a store, saloon, freighting business and cattle ranch. A post office, assigned the name of Turkey, was established in 1903, with Nellis as postmaster.

In 1905, James P. "Jimmie" Cleator arrived at Turkey Creek Station from the gold fields of California. He had been born on the Isle of Man, and worked as a seaman on a clipper ship. He arrived in America in 1889 and eventually worked his way to San Francisco. He came to Arizona around 1900, and in 1905 became Nellis' partner in his various enterprises. By 1907, the town had a population of forty.

In 1909, the partnership of Nellis and Cleator dissolved, with Cleator keeping the store and saloon, and Nellis concentrating on the cattle business. In 1913, Cleator built a new store next to the railroad tracks, and installed a generator to give the town electricity. Nellis retired in 1919, and in 1925 Jimmie Cleator officially changed the name of Turkey Creek Station to Cleator. However, the process of removing the tracks of the Bradshaw Mountain Railway, which had begun in Crown King in 1926, reached Cleator in 1932. With the railroad business gone, the town's population decreased rapidly, and Cleator has hung on since, serving local miners and passing tourists. A rock school house was built in Cleator by the W.P.A. during the 1930s, and is still standing, although it hasn't been used for many years.

There are two ranches in the Cleator area, both of which have passed through many hands over the years. The AY Ranch is located

James P. Cleator
Courtesy Crown King Saloon

about a mile north of Cleator on the Blue Bell Road. It was once the headquarters of the Orr family ranch, and much earlier had been Frank and Bessie Morgan's home. A quarter of a mile down Turkey Creek are the FF Ranch buildings.

This ranch's earliest owners were Marshal Young and his wife Adeline Champie Young, who sold out to Fred and Bill Cordes while the railroad was still running through Turkey Creek Station. Fred and his wife, Claire Champie Cordes, ranched there for several years, but eventually bought some land from Jeff Martin and moved their ranch headquarters to Bumble Bee. The FF buildings are still there, but have not been the ranch headquarters for about fifty years.

Several mines have operated sporadi-

The Cleator General Store.
Courtesy Prescott National Forest

cally over the years near Cleator, and have provided some business for the small town. These mines include the Swastika, at the site of the old Black Warrior and Silver Prince, the DeSoto, and the Thunderbolt, Zika, Silver Cord and French Lilly to the south along Turkey Creek. The Silver Cord was operated as far back as the 1880s, and the claim is now in the name of Tom Cleator, Jimmie's son. During the Great Depression, several miners managed to survive by panning a little gold out of Turkey Creek to the south of Cleator. The remains of their small rock houses can still be found along the creek bank. In the late 1940s the French Lilly was running a fifty-ton mill for twenty-four hours a day, and sixty people were getting their mail in Cleator. The town then consisted of a combination grocery store, service station, saloon, and sixteen houses.

As small as it was, Cleator was the center of business and social activity for the scattered ranches and mines. Dances were held in the rock school house, and locals danced to the sounds of a hand-cranked phonograph player. A violent incident occurred at one of these dances in the 1950s that involved a Cleator citizen who lived in the town for most of the next thirty years. During the height of the dance, Roland St. Louis, who lived on a mine claim just outside of Cleator, decided to deliver a sermon to the party-goers. This was not appreciated, and one of the hands at the AY Ranch volunteered to take St. Louis outside. Once outside, a struggle ensued, and the ranch hand was fatally shot in the head. St. Louis was tried, and sent to the State Hospital in Phoenix. He maintained that he had not intended to hurt anyone, and that the shooting was an accident resulting from a struggle for the gun. He returned to Cleator after a couple years in the hospital, and stayed until the late 1980s. He died shortly after retiring to the Pioneer's Home in Prescott.

One of the most celebrated citizens of Cleator was Jean Darnell, whose picture appeared on the front page of *The Arizona Republic* on March 23, 1984, along with a story about his colorful past. According to this article, stories about him had appeared in the paper many times over the years as he eluded capture after escapes from both the state mental hospital and the federal prison camp on Mount Lemmon. He was known as the "wild man of the mountains" because of his ability to disappear into the wilderness for long periods while on the run from one posse or another. His only crime was his refusal to be drafted

Tommy Cleator

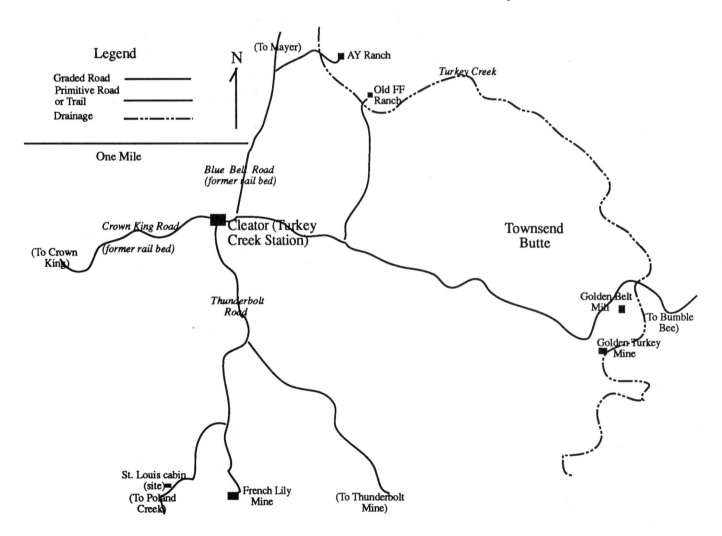

during World War II, which he didn't feel was fair since he had already served in the armed forces back in the twenties. He escaped from the state hospital several times. Darnell did not mind admitting that he often helped himself to whatever food he could find in houses or cabins in the Bradshaws. He had the reputation of being a tidy thief though, and victims, such as Frances Pickett, said they could always tell when Darnell had visited because, although food was missing and things moved around,

the dishes were washed and the kitchen cleaned.

James Cleator died in 1959, and the businesses have since been operated by his son Tom. Other than this, little has changed in Cleator for several decades. Groceries and gas are no longer sold there, but Tommy still runs the small saloon for the thirsty tourists on their way to Crown King, and the few stubborn miners who still have claims in the area.

The Cleator store as it looks today. The store has not been open for years. Only the saloon that was added to the left side of the original building is open occasionally.

Chapter Twenty-Six:
Crown King in the Twentieth Century

A view of downtown Crown King after the arrival of the railroad. The general store is at the extreme left, the railroad depot and water tank in the left foreground, the saloon in the center, and the Tiger Gold Company warehouse on the right. The buildings in the right foreground were houses built as residences for railroad workers. The building in front of the Tiger warehouse contained large oil tanks which supplied oil to both the railroad and the Tiger Gold Company. Courtesy Crown King Saloon

After George Harrington returned to Crown King from Prescott, where he had served as a county supervisor, he settled at the north end of town with his family at the old Crown King mine assay office and company store buildings. Just south of the assay office and above the railroad tracks, a house was built in 1897 for Harrington's son Rube and his new bride Gertrude, or "Maude." Just north of the assay office, Jack Sweet, who married Harrington's daughter Helen, built a small house.

They lived in this house for several years until Rube and Maude moved back to Illinois. Jack and Helen then moved into the "Harrington" house. All of these buildings are still standing, and the only one not now occupied is Jack Sweet's original house, formerly known as the "house that Jack built."

The Harrington's and Jack Nelson, who was married to Harrington's daughter Esther, or "Essie," formed the Nelson Mining Company to operate the Philadelphia Mine, located below the Crowned King Mine in the same drainage. They constructed a narrow gauge rail line from the Philadelphia to the main line in downtown Crown King, so their ore cars could dump directly into the Bradshaw Mountain Railway cars. A shed was built along the line, high on the hillside above the Harrington house, to service the cars. Between the shed and the house, Harrington erected a tent to serve as an office for the company. To complete the Nelson settlement, a house was moved over from the Wildflower Mine in 1914 to serve as a bunkhouse for the mine crews. Later, this became strictly the cookhouse, and a new bunkhouse was built near the ore car shed. It was known as the "Buzzard's Roost," and is now the house of Tony Nelson, a grandson of Jack Nelson. The ore car shed no longer exists, and the rails were torn up long ago, although the line can still be followed through the trees. The cookhouse from the Wildflower is now Dick and Frances Pickett's summer home. Frances Nelson Pickett is one of George Harrington's granddaughters. Her grandmother on her mother's side, Bessie Morgan, once cooked for the Philadelphia crews in the same house. The tent office also still stands, and is Charley Bill Nelson's summer home. The tent has been roofed over and added on to, but the original tent fabric can still be seen on the inside ceiling.

Jack Nelson was born in Sweden and came to America in the 1890s. He had served as a deputy sheriff in Crown King before becoming involved with his father-in-law, George P. Harrington, in the Nelson Mining Company. He suffered a lingering death as a result of a mining accident in which he was struck by a timber, and fell into a mine shaft. While he seemed to recover physically, he had apparently suffered some brain damage and became disoriented. He was taken to the hot baths at Castle Hot Springs, and then sent back to Illinois, but he became so violent that he even tried to kill his wife, Essie. He was hospitalized, but died in 1906 when he was only 42 years old.

True to his reputation, George Harrington became active in the community affairs of Crown King, and was always generous with his money. He donated the land and some of the money for the new Crown King School, and built a non-denominational church in downtown Crown King. Money for the school was also donated by the Santa Fe Railroad, and the Bradshaw Reduction Company. The new school opened in 1917. Classes had originally been held in a boarding house in 1894, but were later moved to the miner's union hall at the lower end of old Crown King. Besides providing the children with a school, the building served as the social center of Crown

The Harrington house.

The Crown King Mine assay office has been a private home for much of this century.

King. Dances were held there once a month, and the women brought sandwiches and made coffee on a campfire outside. It is believed by some, and seems likely, that the school building was originally the schoolhouse in Oro Belle, and was moved to Crown King. Harrington died in Los Angeles in 1922, after being sent there to be treated for cancer. He was probably the most influential and respected man in early Crown King.

After the railroad built its depot, warehouse, and crew quarters in the flat part of Bradshaw Basin in 1904, the old town of Crown King's days were numbered. Many of the saloons had closed after the Crown King Mine had shut down, but a few, those owned by Harry Brown, Ike Patrick, Billy Petrie, and Ed Gobin, formerly of Alexandra, remained open. When the railroad arrived in town, the old businesses were refurbished and a few new ones built. However, the final blow was struck when a great fire reduced most of old Crown King to ashes. Tom Anderson, who later ran the Crown King Saloon for several decades, gave an account of this fire. "When someone yelled 'fire' that day we went to work fast but the town was an inferno before we knew it. It didn't seem to make much difference where we started so we concentrated on a saloon, sixteen feet from a burning store building. I climbed up on the roof and the other guys handed buckets of water up to me. It was hot up there and the smoke was so thick I couldn't see whether the saloon was on fire or not. I could hear men yelling as they came up the hill from new Crown King and I could hear women screaming and the kids running around whooping over the school house being gone. Every once in a while someone would throw me a

The Crown King school.

"Doc" Tyler's Granite Saloon, all that remains of it is a stone foundation on the hillside behind the Crown King General Store. Courtesy Don Van Tilborg

half pint of whiskey which I would consume without taking the bottle from my lips.

"We saved the saloon and that night, much against the owners wishes, we drank its contents."[32]

A general store was built near the railroad depot, and saloons and cabins began to spring up in the area. Old-timer "Doc" Tyler built his Granite Saloon behind the store, and Harrington's Tiger Gold Company built a warehouse and oil storage tanks at the end of the tracks in town. There were also railroad section crews and managers living in various quarters constructed by the railroad company. Other than the depot itself, which collapsed in

a snow storm in 1936, most of these railroad buildings are still standing and in use.

The man who probably lived in Crown King longer than anybody else, came to Arizona from Tennessee in 1897. Tom Anderson started as a miner, working at the Crowned King Mine and mill before it closed, and at the Gladiator with Roscoe Willson. Shortly after the turn of the century, he built a butcher shop where downtown Crown King is now located. In 1916 he moved, or had moved, the saloon from Oro Belle to Crown King. Members of the Harrington family remember that he hired Frank Morgan, who drove the stage from the Oro Belle to Crown King, to haul the building

"Doc" Tyler behind the bar in his Granite Saloon. Courtesy Crown King Saloon

Tom Anderson Courtesy Crown King Saloon

over the steep road, piece by piece. His wife, Bessie, rode with him on many of the trips he made with the burros carrying sections of the saloon.

There is some dispute over who first operated the saloon, then known as a pool hall. There are still tokens in existence issued by Alphonso Caggiano for use in his pool hall, and some believe he was actually the first owner. Before long, however, it became Tom Anderson's pool hall and boarding house, and he also issued tokens for use by his patrons. Tony Nelson thinks that Caggiano may have owed Anderson money, possibly from moving the building, or other carpentry work. Anderson was said to have been an excellent carpenter and furniture maker. He was also a prodigiously strong man, and had apparently been able to do the work of two men while working in the mines. He also had the reputation of being a bit of a bully, and was able to intimidate both adults and children when he wanted to. He ran the pool hall and boarding house, later just the saloon, for thirty-five or forty years, until his death in the mid-1950s. He also built himself a large house on the hillside behind the general store. It burned down in the late 1950s, but the wreckage of it can still be found. He was an accomplished "moonshiner,"

and during prohibition, illicit drinkers were accommodated either at his pool hall, or at the house. The remains of his "wine cellar" can still be seen in the foundation of his house.

Besides serving illicit beverages, Anderson was also not too proud to serve out-of-season game at his boarding house. A game warden became suspicious of him and decided to make an example out of Tom, since many locals survived the Great Depression by eating deer and other game without regard to game laws. The warden followed Tom for a couple days, and finally caught him gutting a deer near the Tiger Mine. He got the drop on him and ordered him to finish butchering the carcass so it could be taken to town and used as evidence against him. Tom did as he was told, but as he was getting ready to leave, he reached down for his jacket and pulled a pistol out of it, turning the tables on the warden. He then made the warden pack the carcass out to his truck and told him to leave the country, and that if he ever saw him again he would kill him. Apparently the warden believed Tom

The Crown King Saloon.

88

The Crown King General Store in an old photograph. Courtesy Crown King Saloon

because he never bothered him again.

Anderson's nearest neighbor was a lady everyone called "Mother" or "Ma" Reed. She lived in a house next to the saloon, and had a few small rental cabins behind her house. She was constantly feuding with Anderson about their property lines, and she sometimes provoked him nearly to the point of blows. She also had a log cabin in a drainage south of town. The cabin no longer exists, but the drainage is now known to the locals as Ma Reed's Gulch. She eventually sold out to "Hop" Manly, who owned the general store at the time. Manly sold the property to Floyd Hambley, who planned to refurbish the house.

While Hambley's brother was repainting the house a cigarette butt was dropped, causing a fire that burned the house and cabins, as well as the church that Harrington had built, which then belonged to Anderson's daughter, Betty. This happened on April 11, 1950, and twenty-two men fought the fire, which burned two acres of pine and brush as well. The fire was so hot that it boiled sap out of the wood in the wall of the general store. The store and Anderson's saloon were barely saved. Ironically, much of the saloon's contents were consumed by the thirsty fire fighters without Anderson's consent.

Another local businessman who did not

Downtown Crown King before the 1950 fire destroyed the church (foreground), and "Ma" Reed's house, between the church and the saloon. Photo is from an old postcard.

89

Robert "Pat" Patterson, Crown King Store owner during the Depression. Courtesy Crown King Saloon

get along with Tom Anderson was Robert "Pat" Patterson, who owned the general store in the 1920s and '30s. He was considered the town patriarch for many years, and during the

Agnes Sorma, later Countess Minotto, in her role as Nora in Ibsen's A Doll's House. Courtesy Frances Pickett

Great Depression, could be counted on to help those in need. He was also a teetotaler and did not approve of Anderson's liquor business, or drinking habits. Matters came to a head during one of the dances held at the schoolhouse. The two men got involved in an argument, and Patterson, who was generally a kind and peaceful man, picked up a chair and hit Anderson over the head with it. Anderson was not hurt seriously, but luckily for Patterson, he was too stunned to continue the fracas.

Another Crown King landmark that no

Countess Minotto in Crown King. Courtesy Tony and Abbie Nelson

longer exists was known as the FF House, since it was once owned by the FF Ranch of Bumble Bee. It was a large two-story house that had been moved up from the Tiger Mine for the Black family in approximately the same period as the relocation of the Saloon from Oro Belle. It was destroyed by a spectacular fire in the the fall of 1976. It stood where the Saloon's rental cabins are now located.

Without a doubt, the most renowned individual ever to live in Crown King was the retired German actress Countess Agnes Minotto. From 1875 to 1910 she was, under her maiden name Agnes Sorma, one of the most

Countess Minotto's house.

famous actresses in Europe. She originated the role of Nora in Ibsen's play *A Doll's House*, and had a tambourine given to her by the playwright with the inscription, "To the most beautiful Nora." During her farewell tour of Europe as Nora, she carried the tambourine with her and wrote on it the cities and dates where she appeared. She then sent it to Ibsen, who had it returned to her after his death.

She had married an Italian Count, and after his death and her retirement from the theater, she moved to Arizona, where her son, James, had a ranch near Walnut Grove. Not wanting to impose on his family, she settled in Crown King in 1926, and had a beautiful stone and wood house built along the old Philadelphia ore car line. In spite of her grand past, she fit in very well with the people of Crown King. Her new neighbors admired her brilliance and intensity, and remembered her for the quantity and quality of the hand embroidery that she was constantly working on. Even though she was in her sixties, she became an avid horsewoman, but during one of her rides in August

of 1926, she was thrown from her horse and seriously injured. A special train was arranged, the last to make the trip to Crown King, to take her to Mercy Hospital in Prescott. While recovering there, she hired one of the nurses, Vivian Yount, to return to Crown King with her and tend to her needs. The Countess apparently recovered completely from her injuries, but a year later, at age 63, she died of heart failure. Her funeral was held in Crown King, but it was snowing so heavily that her son called her friends on the Forest Service telephone, telling them not to attempt the dangerous trip. Nearly everyone in Crown King attended the funeral services, which were conducted by Father Payas, a Catholic priest. She was buried on a knoll near her house, but her son later had her body moved back to Italy to be buried beside her husband. The flattened spot on top of the knoll where she was buried can still be found, ringed by a low stone and masonry wall. Her house is still standing and in use as a summer home. Her nurse, Vivian Yount, married Hugh Nelson, one of Jack Nelson's sons, and remained in Crown King until her death in 1985. One of their sons, Tony, still lives in Crown King with his family.

Vivian Yount Nelson had come from Tennessee, and after she was settled here her mother, Ella, and four brothers and sisters, followed her to Arizona. Ella married a man whose family name is famous in Arizona history. Walter Tewksbury was one of the last survivors of the Graham-Tewksbury feud, known as the Pleasant Valley war. He was only a boy at the time of the violence, but throughout his life, he refused to talk to anybody about his memories of the feud. He married Ella, and settled in a house in Crown King, near to where the Nelson rail line met the Bradshaw tracks. After Walter died in 1945, Mrs. Tewksbury lived in the house alone for years until she moved to Prescott in the late 1960s to live with her daughter. She died in 1974. The Tewksbury house still exists, right next to a tall stone and concrete pier that once supported the last section of the Philadelphia rail line. One of Ella's sons, Everett Yount, worked in the Iron King mine near Humboldt for years, but later moved back to Crown King to work in the local mines, and on his own claims. Everett was one of Crown King's earliest citizens still living there until his death in July of 1990.

The Tewksbury house

Grant Van Tilborg
Courtesy Crown King Saloon

After Tom Anderson died in 1955, his daughter, Betty, sold the Saloon to Grant Van Tilborg, youngest son of Glen and Elsie Van Tilborg. Grant was born in Duncan Camp, Nevada in 1918, shortly before the Van Tilborg's moved to Crown King. He was still too young to go to school when his older brother, Don, commuted from their Towers Mountain ranch to the school in Crown King on a burro. Before buying the ranch in town, the family lived in the two-story building next to the old Harrington assay office. Glen commuted to work at the Lincoln and Swastika mines by foot.

After buying the ranch in Crown King in 1924, the Van Tilborgs became ranchers, but never really got mining out of their blood. Their Forest Service grazing allotment included all of Hell's Hole on its east side, and to the west included Horse Mountain. There was a lot of fence to build in very rugged country, and in the days before metal fence posts, all post holes were dug by hand. After the mining companies had cut down most of the timber in the area to run their mills, and before the oak and manzanita thickets took over, there was a

The old Van Tilborg ranch house.

great deal of grass in Bradshaw Basin, making cattle ranching much more feasible than it would be today. The Van Tilborg's kept the spud ranch on Towers Mountain, and for many years they spent their summers on Towers, and wintered at the ranch in Crown King.

Both Don and Grant had to help with the cattle business, but both spent much of their time mining. Don worked at the Swastika, the Golden Turkey on Turkey Creek, owned the Crown King General Store for a while in the 1940s, and eventually went to work at the mines in Bagdad. He is now retired and living in Crown King. Grant worked the Oro Bella for a time in the 1940s, moving from there to Goodwin, and then to Cleator. After buying the Saloon, he spent most of his remaining years running the only bar in town. For twenty years he was probably the best known and best liked citizen of Crown King. If the town had elected a mayor, he surely would have been it. His style was relaxed, friendly, and trusting. During the day he could usually be found out on the porch of the Saloon, enjoying the mountain air. If you wanted a beer, you just helped yourself and left your money in, or on, the ancient cash register. The back bar was piled high with Grant's ore samples and he made the building something

of a museum by displaying old pictures of the town and its former citizens on the walls. Saturday night dances became a fairly regular tradition, and if a band was not available, he had a couple of ancient jukeboxes to provide the music. Grant finally sold the Saloon in 1975, and died soon after that. The Saloon has passed through several hands since then, but it will certainly never again have the old western style and hospitality that Grant provided.

The town of Crown King has not changed much in the last seventy years. It goes through periods that are relatively more or less quiet than others. The world wars saw an increase in mining activity, as minerals were needed for the war effort, but after the wars, great slumps in demand occurred. During the Second World War, most of the machinery was removed from the mines and mills, to be melted down for the machinery of war. The Great Depression forced many people to scratch out a living from abandoned mines, or pan what gold was left out of the creeks. They lived mainly on what food they could hunt or grow.

The Forest Service has provided some employment over the years, but again, subject to economic ups and downs, as well as changing governmental policies. A new Ranger

Downtown Crown King today, looking past the General Store toward the Saloon. Out of sight between them is the recently built Crown King Volunteer Fire Department building, which is approximately where the church and Ma Reed's houses stood before they burned down in 1950.

Station and house for the District Ranger were built in the 1930s and are still in use. The 28,000 acre Battle Fire in 1972, which was started by campers in Battle Flat, caused a decade-long increase in money allocated to the Crown King Ranger District. Large fire and recreation crews were hired, and local businesses prospered. In 1979, the trend was reversed as the Crown King Ranger District, the oldest in Arizona, was abolished, and

Forest Service jobs have steadily diminished since then. From roughly 1985 to 1988, the old Gladiator Mine was reopened, and a crew of forty to fifty miners was put to work, just after another effort to reopen the Crowned King Mine had ended. The only reliable source of income for businesses in the Bradshaws in the last half century has been tourism, spurred by the construction of the Horse Thief Basin Recreation Area in 1934.

The Crown King Station bar and restaurant is another new structure to downtown Crown King. It is on the site of the former Tie House saloon which burned down in an arson-caused fire in May, 1988. Before being expanded into a saloon and restaurant, the tie house had been a small building built of railroad ties. It had served variously as a blacksmith shop, post office, and cafe.

94

The building at the west end of the street, currently housing "The Prospector" gift shop, started appearing in old photographs of Crown King at the same time as the Saloon. Presumably it was built as a shed or garage for the Saloon, then a pool hall and boarding house. For many years it was an auto repair garage operated by James Manifee, who grew up in Crown King and whose family owns the house behind "Crown King Station." The house was built by the railroad as an employee residence in 1904.

Chapter Twenty-Seven: Horse Thief Basin and Tourism--The Southern Bradshaws Today

Before the invention of air conditioning, the main preoccupation of Phoenix residents was to get to someplace cool, or wet, whenever possible. To answer this need, and to provide work during the Great Depression, the Civilian Conservation Corps constructed the Horse Thief Basin Recreation Area in a wooded basin about five miles southeast of Crown King.

There are many stories about how the basin got its unsavory name. Former Bradshaw resident and historian Roscoe Willson denies that there were ever any horse thieves in the area, and yet, he also tells stories about the horse thieves that gave the basin its name. Willson said that the first resident of the basin was a rancher named Simpson, who lived there in the 1860s and '70s and sold milk, butter, and beef to Bradshaw City and the mines in the area. When he left, a man who came to be known as "Horse Thief" Thompson took over

his log cabin near where the resort is now located. Thompson's vocation was to steal horses from freighters camped for the night along the Black Canyon road. Then, the next day, he would approach the freighters and volunteer to find their horses for a fee. His scam was eventually discovered, and the law made him stop.

Another story is that a rustler named "Horse Thief" Davis established a way station for stolen horses being moved from Utah to Mexico. He was later joined by "Horse Thief" Thompson, but they were both forced to leave when the mountains became more populated.

Claire Champie Cordes, in her self-published book, *Ranch Trails and Short Tales*, wrote that her family, the Champies, used to camp in the basin and knew Thompson. She maintains that the log cabin was located where Horse Thief Lake is now located, and that there was also a corral there to hold the stolen

Cabin in Horsethief Flat, the present location of the tennis courts and playground. This was probably "Horse Thief" Thompson's cabin. Courtesy Prescott National Forest

Civilian Conservation Corps camp in Horsethief Basin.
Courtesy Crown King Saloon

horses. Thompson would go to Phoenix and gather stray horses, which he would herd back to the basin and brand. Once the brand healed, he would take the horses to Prescott and sell them. On his return trip to the basin, he would gather what horses he could find in the Prescott area and repeat the process. He got away with this for quite some time, until someone trailed him and found out what he was doing. He spent some time in prison at Florence, and then settled on Humbug Creek, near the Champie's ranch.

There was never any significant mining activity in Horse Thief Basin, but there is an intriguing story about a lost silver mine in the area. The "Lost" Horse Thief Mine was discovered by Charlie Jones during a ride from Tip Top to Alexandra, where he worked. He discovered a ledge in the northwest part of the basin and asked Ed Gobin, the saloonkeeper in Alexandra, to have the ore assayed while he was on a trip to San Francisco. When Gobin returned, he told Jones that the rock assayed at 600 ounces of silver per ton. Gobin grubstaked

Jones so he could relocate the ledge, but, while returning to the basin, Jones was killed when his rifle was accidentally discharged while he was dragging it through some brush. A com-

Shelter at Hazlett Hollow campground,
built by the CCC's.

panion brought Jones' body back to Alexandra, and the silver ledge was never found.

Other than these stories, little is recorded of the early history of Horse Thief Basin, up until the time that a CCC camp was set up at the present site of the Forest Service guard station in the early 1930s. A 4,000-acre recreation area was built from the ground up. They constructed a rock and masonry dam to form Horse Thief Lake; built three campgrounds, Hazlett, Turney Gulch, and Kentuck Springs; and built a resort with a store, rental cabins, and tennis courts. In 1934, the Forest Service issued the City of Phoenix a Special Use Permit which made the recreation area a Phoenix city park. For years, the basin was a popular place for Phoenicians during the hot summers, in spite of the long drive over a rough dirt road. Several private summer homes were also built in the basin, mainly by families from Phoenix. However, with the advent of air conditioning, and the easier paved-road access to other vacation areas in the state, use of the basin began to decline. In the late 1960s the city returned jurisdiction of

the recreation area to the Forest Service, and the resort was sold to a private party to be operated as a concession on Forest Service land.

With the tremendous growth of the Phoenix metropolitan area in the last thirty years, campers, hunters, and tourists have again discovered Horse Thief Basin, even though it still is not as busy as the more accessible areas of the state. Beyond the facilities in the recreation area, the isolated beauty of the Bradshaw Mountains, and their rich historical heritage have drawn an increasing number of people to the area. Crown King itself has become a popular summer home area, and the whole Bradshaw Basin is becoming crowded with cabins. The prospectors who first followed Poland Creek up into the mountains to find the veins from which the placer gold in Black Canyon came from would be amazed at the changes that 125 years have brought to the once pristine Bradshaws. I hope that this book will help future generations appreciate their historical significance, and preserve their unique beauty and western rural lifestyle.

Horse Thief Lake, formed behind a native rock and masonary dam built by the CCC's.

98

Footnotes

1. W. D. Bradshaw letter from Olive City, N. M., Aug. 1, 1863, *San Francisco Bulletin*, Aug. 24, 1863 in Hayden File, Arizona Collection, ASU.

2. Daniel Ellis Conner, *Joseph Reddeford Walker and the Arizona Adventure* (Norman: University of Oklahoma Press, 1956), pp. 159-160.

3. Miner, Sept. 21, 1864, 2:2.

4. *Weekly Arizona Miner*, Dec. 12, 1868, 2:4.

5. Ibid., Jan. 9, 1869, 3:2.

6. Ibid., June 12, 1869, 3:3.

7. Ibid., Jan. 15, 1870, 2:3.

8. Ibid., Jan. 22, 1870, 3:2.

9. Thomas Edwin Farish, *History of Arizona* (Phoenix: Manufacturing Stationers, 1920), p. 265.

10. *Weekly Arizona Miner*, Aug. 20, 1870, 3:3.

11. Ibid., Feb. 11, 1871, 3:2.

12. Ibid., April, 29, 1871, 2:2.

13. Ibid., May 27, 1871, 3:3.

14. Ibid., June 27, 1879, 4:3.

15. Ibid., March 28, 1879, 4:3.

16. Ibid., June 18, 1880, 4:1.

17. Ibid., May 27, 1881, 2:2.

18. Ibid., Aug. 29, 1879, 2:2.

19. Ibid.

20. Ibid.

21. Ibid., June 9, 1876, 2:2.

22. Ibid., 2:3.

23. Ibid., 3:1.

24. Ibid., June 16, 1876, 3:2.

25 *Prescott Weekly Courier*, Nov. 10, 1883, 1:6.

26. George M. Wheeler, *Preliminary Report of Explorations in Nevada and Arizona* (War Department, 1872), p. 50.

27. *Weekly Arizona Miner*, Sept. 25, 1874, 2:2.

28. Ibid., Oct. 8, 1880, 4:3.

29. *Prescott Weekly Courier,* March 15, 1884, 2:3.

30. Elsie Van Tilborg, Personal Interview

31. Helen Harrington Sweet, *The Bradshaw Mountains: Some Historical Data of Them Compiled by Helen Harrington Sweet,* (Undated manuscript).

32. Tom Anderson, quoted in a letter from Betty Anderson to Roscoe Willson, August 24, 1952, Arizona Historical Foundation Roscoe Willson Collection.

Bibliography

Anderson, Betty. Letter to Roscoe Willson, August 24, 1952. Arizona Historical Foundation. Roscoe Willson Clipping File. Hayden Library. Arizona State University.

Arizona Census. Arizona Historical Foundation. Arizona State University.

Arizona Miner (Prescott)

Daily Arizona Journal-Miner (Prescott)

Weekly Arizona Journal-Miner (Prescott)

The Arizona Republic (Phoenix)

Blandy, John F. "Mining in Yavapai County, Arizona." *The Engineering and Mining Journal.* LXIII, Feb. 27, 1897, p. 212.

Bradshaw, W. D. Letter from Olive City, N. M., Aug. 1, 1863. *San Francisco Bulletin.*, August 24, 1863. Hayden Pioneer Biographical File. Arizona State University.

Cordes, Claire Champie. *Ranch Trail and Short Tales.* Self-published, 1986.

Conner, Daniel Ellis. *Joseph Reddeford Walker and the Arizona Adventure.* Norman: University of Oklahoma Press, 1956.

"Crown King Fire Razes Homes." *Prescott Evening Courier*, April 12, 1950, p. 1.

Crown King History compiled by Crown King School Students in 1957. Crown King Library.

Crown King Ranger District Files.

Duning, Charles H. & Edward H. Peplow, Jr. *Rocks to Riches: The Story of American Mining...Past, Present and Future...As Reflected in the Colorful History of Mining in Arizona, the Nations Greatest Bonanza.* Phoenix: Southwest Publishing Co. Inc., 1959.

Farish, Thomas Edwin. *History of Arizona.* Phoenix: Manufacturing Stationers, 1920.

Granger, Byrd Howell. *Arizona's Names (X Marks the Spot).* Tucson: Falconer Pub. Co., 1983.

Hamilton, Patrick. *The Resources of Arizona.* San Francisco: A. L. Bancroft & Co. 1884. 3rd. ed.

Haury, Emil W. *The Hohokam: Desert Farmers and Craftsmen.* Tucson: University of Arizona Press, 1976.

Hayden Pioneer Biographical File; Arizona Collection, Arizona State University.

Heatwole, Thelma. "Back to Oro Belle." *The Arizona Republic*, July 5, 1970, K1.

Heatwole, Thelma. "Fort Misery trip is one into time." *The Arizona Republic*, February 17, 1972. p. 26.

Helm, P. R. and M. H. Helm. *Yee Fat Jack Group.* Mining Claim Prospectus, 1945

Henderson, Patrick. *A History of the Prescott Bradshaw Mining Districts.* Thesis. Manuscript. University of Arizona, 1958.

Hinton, Richard J. *The Handbook to Arizona.* San Francisco: Payot, Upham & Co., 1878. Republished; Tucson: Arizona Silouettes, 1954.

Johnston, Francis J. *The Bradshaw Trail: Narrative and Notes.* Riverside: Historical Commission Press, not dated.

Lindgren, Waldemar. *Ore Deposits of Jerome and the Bradshaw Mountains.* United States Geological Survey Bulletin. No. 782, 1926.

Manifee, James. Interview with Glen Van Tilborg. May, 1957.

Martin, Vernon. Personal Interview. August 5, 1989.

Phoenix Daily Herald

Pickett, Frances. Personal Interviews, September 2 & 16, 1989.

Prescott Evening Courier

Prescott Weekly Courier

Raymond, Rossiter W. *Mines, Mill, and Furnaces of the Pacific States and Territories: An Account of the Condition, Resources, and Methods of the Mining and Metallurgical Industry in these Regions, Chiefly Relating to the Precious Metals.* New York: J. B. Ford & Co., 1871.

Sayre, John W. *Ghost Railroads of Central Arizona.* Boulder: Pruett Publishing Company, 1985.

Semi-Weekly Breeze. Taylorsville, Illinois.

Simpson, Claudette. "Countess Agnes Minotto." *Westward.* February 11, 1977, pp. 3-5.

Smith, Fred. "Once Upon a Crime." *The Arizona Republic,* 1984.

Sweet, Helen Harrington. *The Bradshaw Mountains: Some Historical Data of them Compiled By Helen Harrington Sweet.* . Manuscript. Crown King Public Library

Sweet, Helen Harrington. Letter to Grant Allen Van Tilborg, April 23, 1957.

Taylor, Glenn. "Town Owner Decides He Needs Rest." *The Arizona Republic,* Dec. 18, 1947, 1:2.

Theobald, John & Lilian. *Arizona Territory Postoffices and Postmasters.* Phoenix: Arizona Historical Foundation, 1961.

Van Tilborg, Donald. Personal Interview, 9/30/84 & 6/11/87

Van Tilborg, Grant (Butch). Personal Interview, August 5, 1989.

Wheeler, George A. *Preliminary Report of Explorations in Nevada and Arizona.* War Department, 1872.

White, Carrietta. "Bumble Bee's Quiet Hive." *Arizona,* May 6, 1984, pp. 18-28.

Willson, Roscoe. "Arizona Days With Roscoe Willson", *The Arizona Republic.* Arizona Historical Foundation. Roscoe Willson Clipping File. Hayden Library. Arizona State University.

Willson, Roscoe. "'Black Yaqui' Kills Herder." *Arizona.* January 15, 1967, pp. 30-31.

Willson, Roscoe. "Last Oldtimer Lives at Crown King Camp." *The Arizona Republic.* September 21, 1952.

Willson, Roscoe. Letter to Ed Fouts. October 12, 1968, Arizona Historical Foundation. Roscoe Willson Clipping File. Hayden Library. Arizona State University.

Willson, Roscoe. Letter to Ralph Crawford, Prescott National Forest Supervisor, July 17, 1966. Arizona Historical Foundation. Roscoe Willson Clipping File. Hayden Library. Arizona State University.

Willson Roscoe. "Oro Belle Strike Around 1905 Recalled." *Arizona,* June 10, 1951, p. II-3.

Willson Roscoe. "Slim Jim, Fat Jack Gave Many a Laugh." *Arizona.* Date Unknown.

Willson Roscoe. "Story of Horsethief Basin in Bradshaw Mountains Recalled." *The Arizona Republic*, April 4, 1948. Arizona Historical Foundation. Roscoe Willson Clipping File. Hayden Library. Arizona State University.

Willson Roscoe. "Two Men's Lives Fill Story of Cleator Town." *The Arizona Republic.* Arizona Historical Foundation. Roscoe Willson Clipping File. Hayden Library. Arizona State University.

Wood, J. Scott. *An Archeological Survey of the Battle Flat Watershed Experimental Chaparral Conversion Project.* USDA Forest Service, 1978.

Workers of the Writers Program of the Work Projects Administration. *Arizona: A State Guide.* New York: Hastings House, 1940.

Yavapai County Records.

Index

ORDER FORM

Mail Orders: Crown King Press, 645 W. Emerald, Mesa, Arizona 85210-4603

Name:_____

Address:_____

City:_____ State:_____ Zip:_____

Price: $16.95 plus sales tax and postage

Number of books ordered:_____

Sales Tax: Arizona residents add 6.5% state sales tax ($18.05)

Postage: Book rate: $1.05 (Total to buy and ship one book - $19.10)

Send check or money order payable to: Crown King Press